Acanthus Press Reprint Series
The 20th Century: Landmarks in Design
Volume 9

Mediterranean Domestic Architecture in the United States

MEDITERRANEAN DOMESTIC ARCHITECTURE IN THE UNITED STATES

REXFORD NEWCOMB

NEW INTRODUCTION BY

MARC APPLETON

ACANTHUS PRESS
NEW YORK 1999

Published by Acanthus Press
54 West 21st Street
New York, New York 10010
E-mail: books@Acanthuspress.com

Library of Congress Cataloging-in-Publication Data

Newcomb, Rexford, 1886-1968.
Mediterranean domestic architecture in the United States / Rexford Newcomb ; with a new introduction by Marc Appleton.
p., cm. – (The 20th century : landmarks in design ; 9)
Originally published: Cleveland, Ohio : Jansen, 1928.
Includes bibliographic references.
ISBN 0-926494-13-9
1. Architecture, Domestic—United States—Spanish influences. 2. Architecture, Domestic—United States—Italian influences. 3. Architecture, Modern—20th century—United States. 4. Architecture, Spanish—United States. 5. Architecture, Italian—United States. I. Title. II. Acanthus Press reprint series. 20th century, landmarks in design ; v. 9.

NA7208.N48 1999
728'.37'0973—dc21 99-040220

Layout by Maggie Hinders

Printed in the USA

INTRODUCTION

THIS introduction to Rexford Newcomb's *Mediterranean Domestic Architecture in the United States* is a somewhat presumptuous one, both because it was never solicited by the author, who died in 1968, and because it is written by a practicing architect who is neither an academic nor a scholar. In my defense, however, I grew up in southern California, familiar with the buildings designed by many of the architects illustrated in Newcomb's book, and over the years they have inspired my own work. Much of my childhood and adolescence were spent exploring and becoming intimate with the house of my maternal grandparents, Mr. and Mrs. Peter Cooper Bryce, designed for them in 1924 by George Washington Smith, one of the pre-eminent eclectic architects represented in the book. While these youthful experiences were of a personal nature, they have enhanced my appreciation for the subject in ways that school and practice cannot.

I. Creating the Myth: A Case Study in Romanticizing the Past

WHEN they journeyed to California from New York on their honeymoon in 1917, my grandparents fell in love with the state and, in particular, with Santa Barbara, where they decided to settle and build a home. During the two or three decades prior to their arrival, Santa Barbara had become an attractive resort town and a haven for the elite, boasting several major hotels and a number of residential estates and villas. During the first few years they rented "Val Verde," the Henry Dater house in Montecito, which had been designed by Bertram Goodhue in 1915 [Fig. 1]. In 1924 they purchased 52 acres on the coast in a then undeveloped area northwest of Santa Barbara called Hope Ranch, and soon

Fig. 1. "Val Verde." Photo by P.C. Bryce, ca. 1922. (Author's collection.)

Fig. 2. "Florestal," P.C. Bryce house. Aerial photo, ca. 1926. (Author's collection)

thereafter hired Smith to design their house, which they named "Florestal" in honor of the extensive gardens and commercial flower business they established there [Fig. 2].

In my conversations over the years with my grandmother and others, it is clear that my grandparents were not easy clients and that they put Mr. Smith and his staff through their paces. In the 1970s, David Gebhard, whose untimely death in 1996 deprived us of what might have been the definitive study of Smith's work,[1] shared with me numerous preliminary sketches and studies for the house from the Smith office archives that the clients had obviously rejected for one reason or another. In researching estate papers following my grandmother's death in 1980, I discovered even more of these [Fig. 3].

Fig. 3. Early schematic design sketches for the P.C. Bryce house by Lutah Maria Riggs, ca. 1924. (Author's collection)

Most of the sketches were drawn by Smith's able young assistant, Lutah Maria Riggs. I gathered that my grandmother was not partial to her and forbade her from attending client meetings, but Riggs managed to exert her influence anyway from behind the scenes. The sketches consist mostly of freehand floor plans, exterior elevations, and renderings of various alternative schemes for the house. They represent a consistently rich and picturesque Spanish architecture inspired mostly by provincial Andalusian examples, and they show that the architect and his clients were struggling to find the right design direction and arrangement for the house. I recall once asking my grandmother what it was like to work with Mr. Smith,

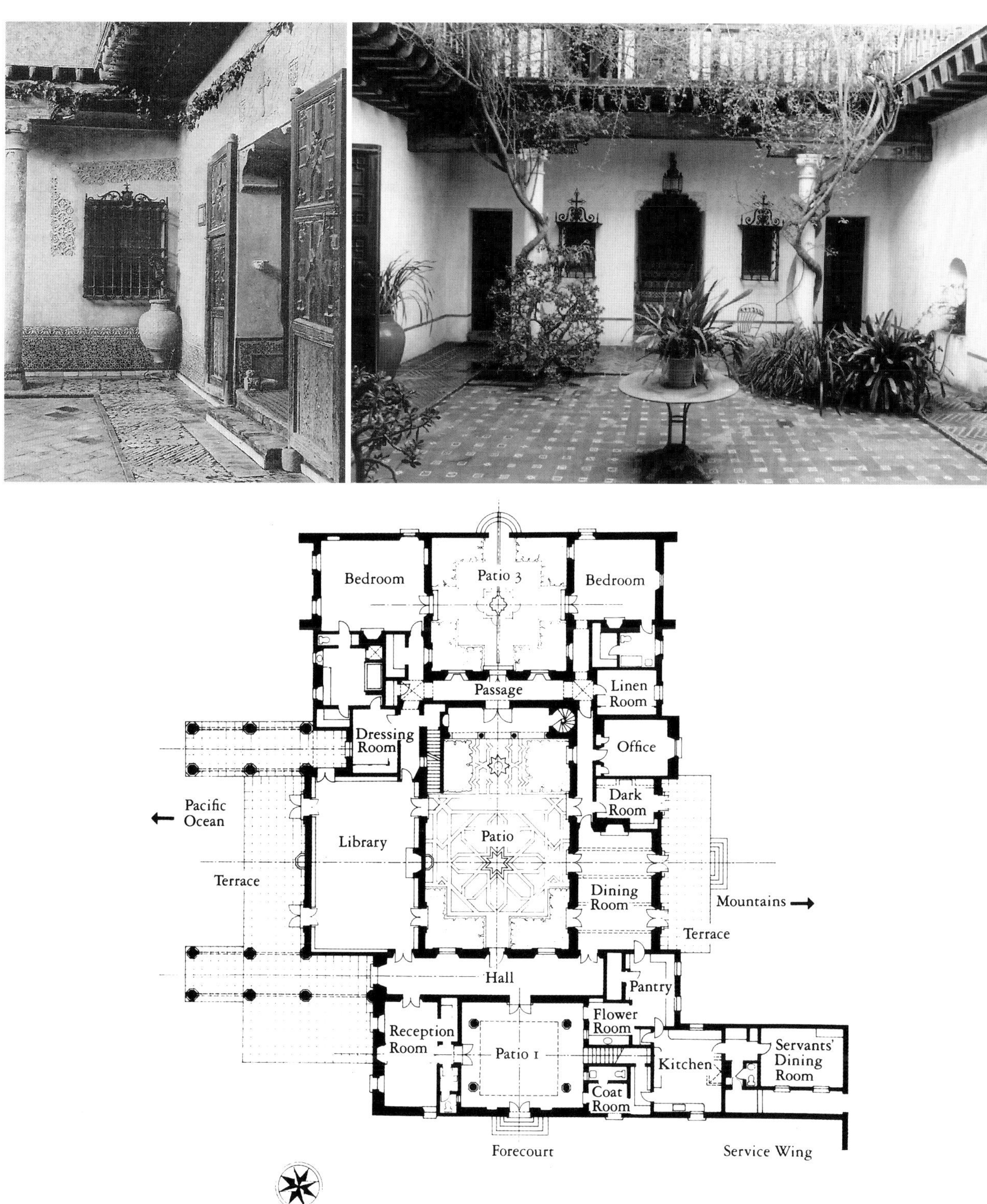

Fig. 4 *(top left).* Entrance patio, "Casa del Greco," Toledo, Spain. From W.L. Bottomley's *Spanish Details*, pl. 13.

Fig. 5 *(top right).* Photo of Entrance Courtyard, P.C. Bryce house. Photo by the author, 1968.

Fig. 6 *(bottom).* Plan, "Florestal," P.C. Bryce house. Drawn by Mark Hewitt from original plans.

expecting an appropriately reverential response. To my great surprise, as if the question had resurrected an irritating memory, she exclaimed in exasperation, "He knew almost nothing about Spanish architecture—I had to show him how to do just about everything!" I accepted this remark with more than a few grains of salt, figuring that my grandmother, who on rare occasions could be rather imperiously dismissive, had probably mistaken as ignorance what most likely was merely Smith's genuinely diplomatic deference to his client. He obviously knew what he was doing, as proven by his success on more than two dozen projects prior to taking this one on for my grandparents, yet it does appear that the final resolution of his efforts in a mutually acceptable plan was indeed hard won.

At least one of the reasons for this difficulty was that my grandmother had rather strong preconceptions about both the design and detailing of the house. In the mid-1920s, before the house was built, she made her own pilgrimage to Spain, and during that trip she began purchasing and collecting materials, fixtures, and various architectural elements for her future home. These included almost all of the glazed ceramic and glass tiles, the wooden doors and shutters, decorative wrought iron grills, and many of the light fixtures. In addition, she had taken photographs and collected postcards of a number of Spanish buildings she visited and admired in the course of her travels. Among these, which I also discovered carefully preserved with captions in one of her old scrapbooks, was the entrance patio of El Greco's house in Toledo, Spain. It is undoubtedly not only the inspiration for but the very model she insisted on for the entrance courtyard of her house, down to and including the carved wooden doors and the detail on the ends of the balcony corbels [Figs. 4 & 5]. The extensive use of interior patios at Florestal (there were three altogether, which functioned as both outdoor living areas and circulation between the rooms) was at the time a new development in Smith's planning, one not apparent in the early sketches and one that I am convinced owed a great debt to the strength and persistence of my grandmother's own convictions [Fig. 6].

She was not the only client in southern California to want a Spanish house, as Newcomb's book shows, and one message I carried away from this anecdote was that "The Creation of a New Spain in America," to borrow the title of a Santa Barbara bicentennial exhibition,[2] was not just the product of a number of dedicated architects practicing between 1915 and 1930 but was the realization of the shared vision and aspirations of their clients, who were generally emigrants escaping from eastern cities to the warmer climates of areas like California in search of a new Eden. To be sure, the original missions and adobes already contained traces of the earlier Spanish colonization, and the land and the sunny climate of California's southern coast provided a suitably hospitable environment. Yet it seems that the real force behind this Mediterranean revival was unencumbered by any allegiance to local history or weather and depended instead on the romantic fantasies of the early twentieth-century newcomers, who looked for their models not so much to the surviving examples of local Spanish Colonial architecture but to their original European precedents.

In a 1967 article in the *Journal of the Society of Architectural Historians*, David Gebhard, who perhaps more than any other individual was responsible for preserving and publicizing California's rich architectural legacy, identified two phases of the revival of Spanish Colonial architecture in southern California: the Mission Revival and the Mediterranean Revival.[3] The two styles were not necessarily exclusive; their chronology overlapped and both were essentially mythic recreations, based only loosely on the original Spanish Colonial architecture of Mexico, the Southwest, and California.

During the Mission Revival phase, from the 1890s to roughly 1915, the most notable buildings tended to be public rather than private: churches, railroad stations, banks, and hotels, rather than houses. While the Mission style seems to have proved less adaptable to residential uses, the reasons for its surrender to the Mediterranean Revival phase, roughly from 1915 to 1930, are not entirely clear. The Mission style was a local and less exotic phenomenon. Perhaps its heavier rhythms and plasticity, the very qualities one might assume would have assured its success, presented an architecture too amorphous and plain to ultimately appeal to more sophisticated clients and their architects. The Mediterranean Revival, however, which drew from a broader range and scale of influences from different European sources, proved admirably suited to residential as well as commercial applications and ultimately prevailed. It was a revival not of indigenous or local architectural traditions but one inspired by far-off Spanish and Italian examples that caught the fancy of the affluent, educated travelers who settled in California after the turn of the century.

Compatible with the importation of foreign architectural influences was the cultivation of a landscape of largely foreign plant varieties that fit a "Mediterranean" setting. The citrus, olive, cypress, eucalyptus, palm tree, and other plants we have come to associate with southern California were in fact all imported to what, by nature, is a desert environment. It has been estimated that approximately 90 percent of the vegetation prevalent today is not native but nevertheless thrives simply by the addition of an unnatural amount of irrigation. Not coincidentally, water has been imported to southern California at great expense from hundreds of miles away in order to keep this "Mediterranean" paradise alive and green.[4]

As we have noted, the new settlers were not pioneers in the traditional American sense but relatively sophisticated tourists who decided to stay on in this paradise. They would make new lives by adopting a new lifestyle in a place that, while civilized and safe, was still foreign and exotic enough to invite the indulgence of their dreams. Most homebuilding, after all, invariably involves a paradoxical search for security stirred by adventure. To help them in this endeavor, they hired equally sophisticated architects who were knowledgeable about European architecture or educated in the Beaux Arts tradition, many of whom had also come west from similar backgrounds and who had the same dreams. As Gebhard observed in an essay on the architect Wallace Neff, "with the majority of architects and clients of the '20s and '30s, there was an overall desire to immerse oneself in some romantically conceived episode of the distant past or to be magically transported to some exotic, faraway place."[5] My grandparents were well-educated, cosmopolitan, upper-class New Yorkers with long-standing family roots in that part of the country. One might imagine they had no business leaving all this to move across the continent and assume a new "Spanish" identity, but they did, willingly inspired and wholeheartedly captivated by the notion that they could start over by reinventing another heritage for themselves. So complete, so sensitively understood and richly detailed was the result, that only a generation later we grandchildren easily accepted Florestal as our true ancestral home, timeworn, beautifully overgrown, and full of latent memories.

Henry James wrote, "If the picturesque were banished from the face of the earth, I think the idea would survive in some typical American breast."[6] There is a palpable, almost visceral quality to many of the architectural renderings by the architects of the Mediterranean Revival that captures this sentiment. It is impossible to look at sketches by Wallace Neff, Winsor Soule, or Lutah Maria Riggs and not appreciate the contrast of bright sunlight and deep shadow or feel the rough presence of the original inspiration [Fig. 7]. Even though these images were designed far from their original homeland, they became something convincingly real in the hands of the better architects. James also observed of California that it seemed "a sort of prepared but unconscious Italy, the primitive *plate,* in perfect condition, but with the impressions of History all yet to be made."[7] Until I was old enough to understand, I never questioned the legitimacy of my grandparents' and Smith's invention but grew up feeling a tangible sense of security in my family's mythical heritage, not in its actual New England past but in its Mediterranean reincarnation in this new "old" place overlooking the Pacific Ocean.

Fig. 7. Sketch for the Burke residence by Lutah Maria Riggs, 1922. (Courtesy of the Architectural Drawing Collection, University Art Museum, University of California, Santa Barbara)

II. Documenting and Promoting the Myth

Many others had preceded my grandparents to Santa Barbara, and for Americans this kind of uprooting experience is perhaps not unusual. Indeed, we are a mixed society of immigrants, by choice and by force. We have, not surprisingly, borrowed most of our architectural inspiration from elsewhere—largely from Europe—along with the rest of the cultural, social, religious, and technological baggage of our forebears. With the exception of Native American Indian settlements, which have claimed the wilderness less destructively and more gracefully, architecture in the United States is a manifestation of more recent and intrusive hybrids. Colonial settlers brought European precedents to civilize New England. Even the original eighteenth-century Spanish Colonial architecture of California and the Southwest, despite having acquired a place in our architectural history that might be considered indigenous, substantially owed its origin and existence to influences brought by the Spanish Conquest.

What was not so easily explained, however, and what my grandparents' new life in Santa Barbara offered only a glimpse of, was the widespread appeal and almost meteoric rise in popularity of the Mediterranean Revival during the 1920s in California and to some extent in Florida. To quote Gebhard again: "In the twentieth century American architectural scene, there has been only one brief period of time and only one restricted geographic area in which there existed anything approaching a unanimity of architectural form. This was the period, from approximately 1920 through the early 1930s, when the Spanish Colonial or the Mediterranean Revival was virtually the accepted norm in Southern California."[8] Its appeal heralded an extremely popular and important change in the architectural landscape of the early twentieth century, and the style continues to affect us to this day. The Revival even found popularity in some fairly unlikely parts of the country, but in states where the climate was relatively temperate, like Florida and California, ambitious developments and even whole communities were planned and designed around Mediterranean themes. Many have been subsequently diluted by the march of progress, a loosening of design controls, and overpopulation, but communities such as Santa Barbara, Ojai, Rancho Santa Fe, and Palos Verdes have continued to enforce their adopted heritage and new real estate developments still commonly establish design guidelines based on these precedents. In the 1920s, the Revival became a craze of significant proportions: it was celebrated in dozens of newspaper and magazine articles and spawned numerous books, among them Newcomb's remarkable and eclectic work reprinted here.

Among the earlier books that had anticipated and then contributed to this trend were the late nineteenth-century grand tour travel books and artistic journals extolling the picturesque virtues of the provincial European countryside, culture, and architecture, especially of Italy, Spain, and France, which were considered even then to be threatened by progress. In my library are several of these books, including a copy (originally belonging to George Washington Smith) of M. Digby Wyatt's *An Architect's Notebook in Spain* (1872), and A.C. Michael's *An Artist in Spain* (no date), illustrated with pen-and-ink sketches and watercolors respectively. The increasing use of photographic illustrations after the turn of the century prompted an even wider public distribution of picture books and portfolios that documented historic European architecture. Of the many books on Spanish architecture from this period, those by Arthur and Mildred Stapley Byne are perhaps best known. A few of the Bynes' books were published by The Hispanic Society of America, an organization founded in 1904 by aficionados of things Spanish and responsible for more than 200 monographs and exhibitions.

Magazines such as *The Western Architect, The Craftsman, The Architect and the Engineer,* and *Pacific Coast Architect* published a variety of articles that featured contemporary American Spanish and Mediterranean revival architecture. The first and most significant books to exclusively collect and copiously illustrate examples it of were published in the mid-1920s beginning with R.W. Sexton's *Spanish Influence on American Architecture* (1926) and followed by Newcomb's *The Spanish House for America* (1927), his *Mediterranean Domestic Architecture in the United States* (1928),[9] and Philip H. Staats's *California Architecture in Santa Barbara* (1929).[10] Once widely read and accessible, these books, like most of the publications of the era, have regrettably become all too scarce.

Some practicing architects today regard rare and out-of-print architectural books as archeological finds to be treasured for the rich sources of inspiration that the books provide to their own work. My office library is full of such books, acquired over the last thirty years, some inherited or received as gifts, others discovered on the dusty shelves of used bookstores for a bargain, and many ordered from specialized booksellers at what always seemed to be outrageously extravagant prices. I admit to being addicted to them and belong to that group of practitioners that assumes a literary foundation for our profession, one based on the study of historic precedents. I believe that the mere presence of these hallowed tomes on our desks imbues our work with cultural connections that cannot be achieved by perusing the latest professional magazines and publications. Their inspirational qualities lift our profession from the popular conventions and fashions of the day and enrich its context, acknowledging the evolution that links us to the past.

Long past their moment in the spotlight, such books now appear only on expensive rare book lists for the cognoscenti, but in their day most of them were published as practical source books that were directed not at amateur bibliophiles like me but to a popular audience of prospective homeowners and their architects and contractors. Like many of today's publications, some were blatantly self-serving architectural monographs; others were more subtle promotional ventures, often subsidized by major manufacturers or suppliers in the construction industry. Two of my favorite out-of-print acquisitions, for example, are a pair of beautifully bound collections of travel photographs of Spain by the architect Richard S. Requa, titled *Architectural Details, Spain and the Mediterranean* (1927) and *Old World Inspiration for American Architecture* (1929).[11] Both were paid for by the Portland Cement Co. of Los Angeles, a major supplier of the key ingredient to both the structural foundations and cement plaster walls that typified Spanish architecture, and a business that obviously stood to profit from any proliferation of the style.

Coincidentally, books like *Mediterranean Domestic Architecture in the United States* were for their time not much different than the so-called "style" books of today that populate our coffee tables, books that our clients are fond of bringing to their meetings with us. These books, both today's and their early twentieth-century precursors, are basically design and architectural surveys that celebrate and promote particular styles. Both intend to indulge our romantic fantasies. An objective study of many of Newcomb's books will also confirm their essential commercial bent, as they did a great deal to advertise and popularize Mediterranean Revival architecture.

III. Rexford Newcomb and the Legacy of the Myth

Rexford Newcomb [Fig. 8] was born in 1886 in Independence, Kansas, and was raised in Burlington, sixty miles to the north, where he received his early schooling.[12] In 1908, after two years at the University of Kansas, he registered at the University of Illinois to pursue studies in architecture, graduating in 1911. Later that year he married and moved to California, where he opened an architectural practice. It does not appear, however, that his professional practice was nearly as active as his teaching and other activities: in 1912 he organized and taught an architectural curriculum at Long Beach Polytechnic's adult education program, which had 3,500 evening students. During the same period, he studied and taught at the University of Southern California in Los Angeles, where he obtained an A.B. degree in sociology and political science.

Fig. 8. Rexford Newcomb. (Photo courtesy of the University of Illinois at Urbana-Champaign Archives)

In 1917, Newcomb accepted an appointment to the faculty at Texas Agricultural and Mechanical College and within a year rose to head the History of Architecture department. In 1918, the University of Illinois awarded him an M. Arch. degree, and later the same year he accepted an offer to join the institution as assistant professor of architectural history. By 1921 he had become a full professor, and in 1931 he was asked to organize and chair the University's College of Fine and Applied Arts, of which he was appointed Dean, a position he held until his retirement twenty-two years later in 1954.

Throughout his career as an educator, Newcomb researched, wrote, and published eighteen books and numerous articles, many of which focused on the history of regional architecture in the United States.[13] In 1916, he published *The Franciscan Mission Architecture of Alta California*, a relatively scholarly and historical work, but *The Spanish House for America* and *Mediterranean Domestic Architecture in the United States* surveyed contemporary American examples of domestic Spanish and Mediterranean revival architecture that he obviously intended as relevant prototypes for prospective clients, homebuilders, developers, and their architects. *The Spanish House for America* presents and discusses various aspects and details in architectural and construction terms that are accessible to the potential homebuilder. *Mediterranean Domestic*

Architecture, a somewhat more ambitious and broader survey, is not as obviously structured and contains significantly less discussion.

The entire text of the original edition of *Mediterranean Domestic Architecture* is a scant eight pages of large print. Given Newcomb's academic credentials, it seems oddly cursory and superficial, presenting only the most general explanations of the history, popularity, and appropriateness of various forms of contemporary Mediterranean architecture to the regions in which they had begun to flourish. It makes a few casual observations about red tile roofs, stucco walls, courtyards, patios, fountains, arcades, iron grillwork, and other salient features. Otherwise, the book's profuse illustrations demonstrate that its intention seems to have had less to do with documenting architectural history than celebrating a popular style of architecture and promoting the work of the architects who were practicing it.

If we look more closely at Newcomb's career, including his civic and community service, the secular nature of his perspective is not surprising. While he was a university professor and a dean, he was nevertheless a practical man who championed the application of art and science for the welfare of the general public. His classes seemed to have had as much to do with home economics as with architectural history, and apparently they were attended by many women. One of his books is dedicated "to that now numerous band of splendid and loyal young women who in bygone years have been members of the author's classes in Home Architecture."[14] In 1934 he organized the Illinois Bureau of Community Planning, which advised the state's communities on their planning and development of physical facilities, and for years he was a member of the Illinois State Planning Commission. He also formed a long-lasting relationship with members of the ceramic tile industry, first with the Associated Tile Manufacturers of America and subsequently the Terra Cotta Service Bureau, the Decorator's Supply Company of Chicago and the Kohler Company. The majority of his publications were addressed not to scholars but to popular and professional audiences. Some were overtly "how-to" books and were subtitled accordingly: *Home Architecture: A Textbook for Schools and Colleges and A Manual for the Home Builder and Home Owner*; *The Colonial and Federal House: How to Build an Authentic Colonial House*, and *The Spanish House for America: Its Design, Furnishing and Garden.*" To his great credit, Newcomb successfully avoided the ivory tower elitism that prevents many academics from reaching a more public forum.

It is not only the practicality of his scholarship that endears Newcomb to the working architect, but his method: in *The Colonial and Federal House*, Newcomb expressed his *modus operandi* as including both "the antique and the modern," both the historical precedent and the contemporary example it could inspire. Architecture was to be appreciated as a continuum, its periods not isolated moments but cycles in a grander historical process. He lamented that the industrialized world had led to a decline in taste and believed that remembering history and precedent could "elevate the tone of home architecture" and help reintroduce the noble tradition of "fine old native handcrafts" to our lives.[15] For him, this dynamic held true for all domestic architecture, Spanish and Mediterranean as well as Colonial and Federal. As a non-practicing architect and a lifetime student of architecture, he looked to those fellow architects whose ongoing work best demonstrated his beliefs. In the contemporary practitioners of the Mediterranean Revival, he found real proof of their validity.

Mediterranean Domestic Architecture in the United States illustrates examples of contemporary houses in the Mediterranean style—some of them newly built—by more than two dozen architects practicing at the time. The majority of the houses are located in southern California and Florida, although there are a few wayward examples in Texas, Kansas, Alabama, Tennessee, Ohio, and Pennsylvania.[16] Floor plans are typically included, along with photographs of each of the houses, welcome additions for today's student of history, but indicative then of the author's intent to provide his readers with useful information for their own designs.

Among the architects featured are some of the Mediterranean Revival's most capable practitioners: in California: George Washington Smith (with nine entries), Wallace Neff, Reginald D. Johnson, and Marston, Van Pelt & Maybury (each with six), and Elmer Grey (four); in Florida, Kiehnel & Elliott (six), Marion Sims Wyeth (five), and Robert L. Weed (four). A few of the architects are no longer familiar names even to the most ardent students of architectural history. Others, like Myron Hunt, Gordon B. Kaufmann, and Roland E. Coate, are regrettably underrepresented. A fair number who should have been included were left out altogether—Addison Mizner and Maurice Fatio in Florida, and James Osborne Craig, Carleton Winslow, Sr., John Byers, Lillian J. Rice, Edwards and Plunkett, William Templeton Johnson, and Mead & Requa in California, to name a few. Surveys can never be complete, however, and besides, everyone inevitably has his or her own favorites to the exclusion of others.

The quality of the architecture shown ranges from elegant to mundane, as was perhaps fitting for such a practical and democratic collection. Although many estate-type houses are included, others appear to be more affordable and not beyond the reach of the middle-class reader, clearly an important consideration for the civic-minded Newcomb.[17] In some cases, a tendency to mix elements from different Mediterranean sources is apparent, a trait reminiscent of the "melting pot" interpretation of the history of the United States. To Newcomb, this was a natural result of the Americanization of Mediterranean influences: "Spanish, Italian, Moorish, Byzantine—Mediterranean types generally—instead of being kept archeologically segregated, are under this orchestral process merged, as were those golden threads of long ago, into a new sun-loving style which, while eminently American in its plan and utilities, is never-the-less distinctly Mediterranean in its origins and spirit."[18]

The inclination to "mix" seemed especially characteristic of the architects of the opulent mansions of Florida resort areas such as Palm Beach and Boca Raton. A key distinction between the work of Addison Mizner and George Washington Smith, for example, rests largely in how promiscuous the former was, and how discriminating the latter with regard to their original sources. The popular appeal of Mediterranean architecture for many residential applications in the United States, however, did not depend on the dazzle of the more richly ornamented or flamboyant combination of styles typical of some of the wealthier homes, but rather on a picturesque simplicity. In *Spanish Influence on American Architecture*, Sexton noted that "the peasant dwelling, or farmhouse of Spain, offers, perhaps, most for adaptation to American needs. Its chief characteristic lies in a pleasing combination of simplicity and dignity. Symmetry is an unknown quantity with Spanish architects."[19] It is this same quality that Gebhard praised in the work of George Washington Smith, referring to its directness and simplicity and its "strong sense of the primitive."[20]

Related to these characteristics was the informality of the architectural floor plans of the Spanish precedents. As Sexton notes, an attractive advantage for residential architects was that these prototypes encouraged an acceptable asymmetry in planning. While the development of the plan in Mediterranean Revival architecture involved the use of conventional formal, discrete spaces or rooms, as in the classical tradition, they were often shifted off axis and informally and asymmetrically arranged. This device offered an opportunity to take maximum advantage of the site, to give the rooms different orientations and views, and to encourage a variety of connections to the surrounding landscape. Examples of this are the Scripps-Booth residence (p.34), the Parshall residence (p. 61), the Eichheim residence (p. 68), and the Rew residence (p. 79). Although it is not included, James Osborne Craig's Hoffmann residence in Santa Barbara exhibits a similarly asymmetrical configuration [Fig. 9]. A related planning device, also borrowed from Mediterranean prototypes, was the lateral extension of the plan, which allowed parts of the house to be a single room in depth—permitting these rooms to be open to the exterior on both sides. Variations of this stretched-out planning are the Semple residence (p. 14), the Parkinson residence (p. 93), the Bourne residence (p. 94), and the Wheeler residence (p. 127). The Peshine house in Santa Barbara by Myron Hunt is another well-known example [Fig. 10].

Whatever planning considerations were at stake, the picturesque characteristics of the Mediterranean Revival finally succeeded in the realized architecture because of what Newcomb recognized as a critical marriage between design and fine craftsmanship. Both knowledge and skill have always been required for revivalist architecture, and quality was possible only because of the

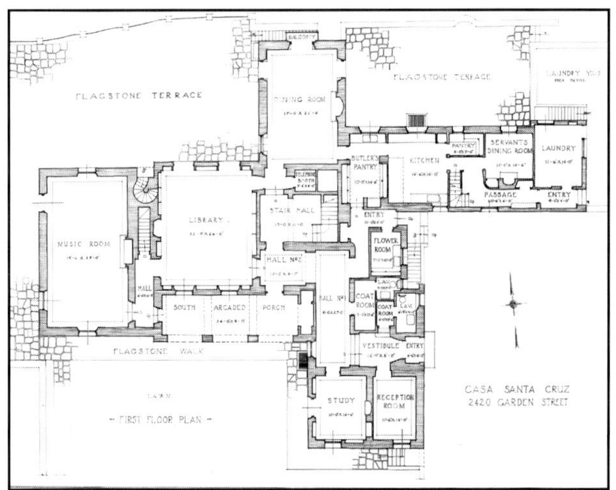

Fig. 9. Plan, Hoffmann residence, ca. 1921. (Courtesy of the Architectural Drawing Collection, University Art Museum, University of California, Santa Barbara)

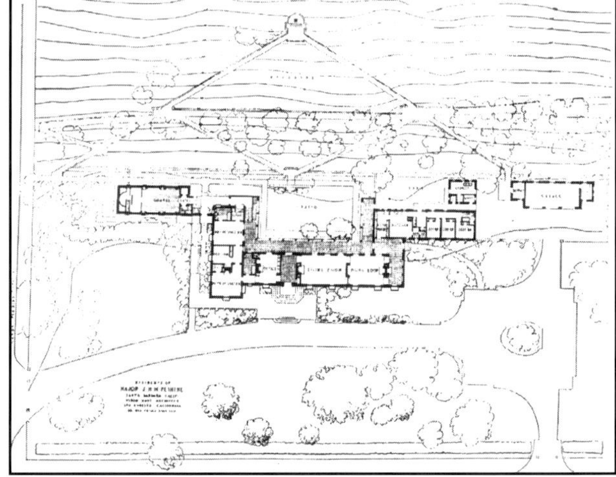

Fig. 10. Peshine house, 1918. *The Architect and Engineer* 56, June 1919.

harmonious working relationships and understanding among client, architect, draftsman, contractor, and the craftsmen involved in realizing the end product. The importance of the attention to materials and details is readily apparent in the better examples of the eclectic architecture of the period, and some of the working drawings that survive hint at what was certainly a prodigious quantity of sketched details and shop drawings, most of them probably jettisoned at the completion of construction after they had served their purpose [Figs. 11, 12 & 13].

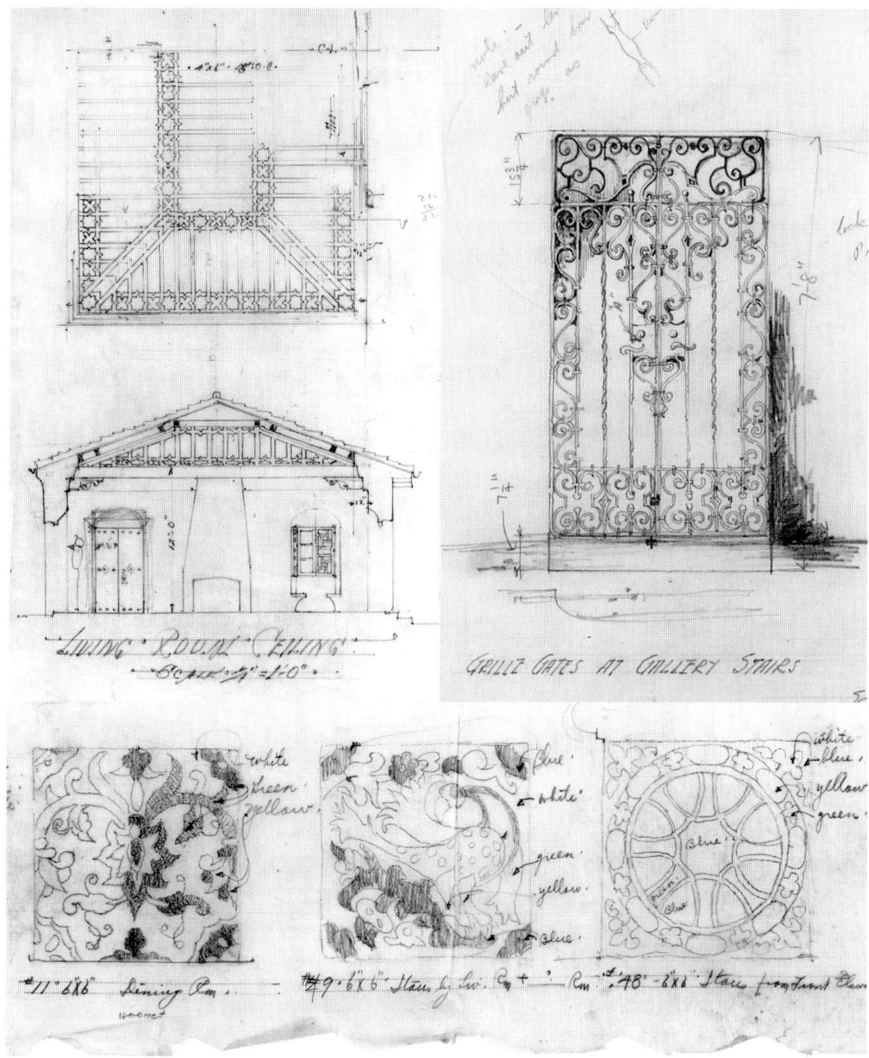

Fig. 11 *(upper left)*. Ceiling Plan, Vincent Residence By George Washington Smith, 1923. (Courtesy of the Architectural Drawing Collection, University Art Museum, University of California, Santa Barbara)

Fig. 12 *(upper right)*. Design for wrought iron gate for the Hoffman Residence By James Osborne Craig, 1921. (Courtesy of the Architectural Drawing Collection, University Art Museum, University of California, Santa Barbara)

Fig. 13 *(bottom)*. Ceramic Tile Designs, Vincent Residence. By George Washington Smith, 1923. (Courtesy of the Architectural Drawing Collection, University Art Museum, University of California, Santa Barbara)

Still vital during the 1920s, the decline of craftsmanship in construction was imminent. Dictated by the machine-made and the mass-produced, the Modern movement, or International Style, soon became a predominant force in the architecture of the United States and other technologically advancing nations. Several historians and critics, including Gebhard, have suggested that the simplicity and purity of abstraction inherent in the work of a few of the Mediterranean Revival architects actually presaged the modern movement. This was probably the case with the architecture of Irving Gill or Bertram Goodhue but not with the work of George Washington Smith or Wallace Neff. It is only in retrospect that later critics have tried to rationalize the presence of proto-Modern characteristics, and these claims appear specious. Smith's work was brilliantly original, but it was always faithful in spirit and detail to its Mediterranean sources. And although Neff experimented with industrialized housing and with new reinforced concrete construction technologies in his "Bubble House," these were separate projects driven by a different muse altogether and this never influenced the romantic and picturesque qualities that distinguished his other residential commissions. The modern movement, assisted no doubt by the Depression, was essentially defined by the technology of the machine and a conscious search for an unprecedented imagery. Conversely for Mediterranean Revival architects, as Newcomb observed, a love for handmade crafts lay at the heart of their enterprise, which was consciously seeking a connection with the past.

As we hurtle towards the millennium, Modernism and its descendants, including that desperate and unraveled cousin labeled "deconstructivism," still dominate the architectural scene, but we are discovering that they have not left us with as rich or humane a legacy as promised. Ironically, of all the stylistic impulses that have had an impact on southern California, the Mediterranean is still the most enduring prototype for both residential and commercial buildings. Whatever criticism can be leveled at the architectural quality of today's revivals—and hackneyed examples most certainly abound—the Mediterranean idiom has survived where others have not. Although originally an imagined tradition, perhaps it has become in time a real one, at least a vernacular if not an indigenous language, a dialect of the mother tongue. The republication of this book serves to remind us that after almost a century, it continues to attract and delight our sensibilities.

Marc Appleton
January 1999
Los Angeles, California

NOTES

1. For many years, Professor Gebhard had reportedly been working on a definitive book on Smith, but, according to his widow, no completed manuscript was discovered at the time of his death. In 1964, Gebhard mounted an exhibition of Smith's work for the Art Gallery of the University of California, Santa Barbara, and a small catalogue from that exhibition was published as *George Washington Smith, 1876–1930: The Spanish Colonial Revival in California*. Santa Barbara, California: University of California, Art Gallery, 1964.
2. David Gebhard, *Santa Barbara: The Creation of a New Spain in America*, Santa Barbara, California: University of California, University Art Museum, 1982 (Catalogue from the Exhibition).
3. David Gebhard, "The Spanish Colonial Revival in Southern California (1895–1930)," *Journal of the Society of Architectural Historians*, vol. 26, May 1967, pp. 131–147.
4. For a good introduction to the politics of water in the American west, see Marc Reisner's *Cadillac Desert*, New York: Viking, 1986.
5. David Gebhard, "Regionalism and Romance" in Jay Belloli *et al*, *Wallace Neff 1895–1982*. San Marino, California: The Huntington Library, 1989 p. 43.
6. Henry James, *Transatlantic Sketches*, 1875.
7. Ibid.
8. David Gebhard, *George Washington Smith 1876-1930: The Spanish Colonial Revival in Southern California*, Santa Barbara, California: University of California, Santa Barbara, Art Gallery, 1964, p.1.
9. It appears that *Mediterranean Domestic Architecture in the United States* may have been first published, or at least scheduled to be published, in 1926, as there is already a reference to it in the bibliography of Newcomb's *The Spanish House for America* of 1927.
10. In 1925, a major earthquake devastated much of Santa Barbara, taking an especially heavy toll on many of the masonry buildings. The city's Plans and Planning Committee was instrumental in encouraging and enforcing a Spanish style in the rebuilding effort, and Staat's book was actually commissioned by Pearl Chase and Bernard Hoffmann of the Committee as a source book to promote the continued architectural development of the city according to acceptable Spanish Revival guidelines. See Gebhard's "Introduction to the New Edition" of 1990.
11. In the foreword to this book, the author states that his "main purpose in the preparation of this work was to provide worthy examples of old world architecture that will stimulate the development of appropriate styles in America."
12. The biographical information on Newcomb is based on a 1954 typewritten description from the Newcomb Archives at the University of Illinois at Urbana-Champaign and on an obituary published March 18, 1968.
13. For a more complete listing, see the Chronological List of Publications by Rexford Newcomb.
14. Rexford Newcomb, *Home Architecture*, New York: John Wiley & Sons, 1932.
15. Rexford Newcomb, *The Colonial and Federal House*, Philadelphia: J.B. Lippincott Co., 1933.

16. The inclusion of these stray examples is somewhat suspect, as they were the exception rather than the norm and probably are misleading in expanding the domain of the Mediterranean Revival to these extremes. In his 1927 *Spanish Influence on American Architecture and Decoration* (New York: 1926), R.W. Sexton further stretched the territory by adding instances in Oklahoma, Maryland, Washington D.C., New Jersey, New York, Rhode Island, and Massachusetts.

17. Despite the overwhelming prevalence in publications of larger, single-family homes, the Mediterranean Revival also had a significant impact on urban apartment houses and other more affordable alternatives. For excellent examples, including projects by F. Pierpont and Walter S. Davies and Arthur B. Zwebell, see *Courtyard Housing in Los Angeles*, Stefanos Polyzoides *et al*, and *Small House Designs*, Carleton M. Winslow and Edward Fisher Brown, eds.

18. Rexford Newcomb, *Mediterranean Domestic Architecture in the United States*, J.H. Jansen, Cleveland, 1928, p. 4.

19. R.W. Sexton, *Spanish Influence on American Architecture and Decoration*, New York: Brentano's, 1927, p. 10.

20. David Gebhard, "Founding Father: George Washington Smith," *Santa Barbara Magazine*, July/August 1993, p.23.

CHRONOLOGICAL LIST OF PUBLICATIONS BY REXFORD NEWCOMB

Books

Franciscan Mission Architecture of California. New York: Architectural Book Publishing Co., 1916.

Outlines of the History of Architecture, Parts I, II & III. Mimeographed and printed, Ann Arbor: Edwards Brothers, 1922, 1923 & 1925.

The Old Mission Churches and Historic Houses of California: Their History, Architecture, Art, and Lore. Philadelphia: J.B. Lippincott, 1925.

The Spanish House for America: Its Design, Furnishing, and Garden. Philadelphia: J.B. Lippincott Company, 1927.

Mediterranean Domestic Architecture in the United States. Cleveland, Ohio: J.H. Jansen, 1928.

In the Lincoln Country. Philadelphia: J.B. Lippincott Company, 1928.

Evolution of the American Farm House. St. Joseph, Michigan: 1929.

Modern Tendencies in Architecture. Hollywood, California: 1930.

Home Architecture: A Textbook for Schools and Colleges / A Manual for the Home Builder and Home Owner (with William A. Foster). New York: John Wiley & Sons Inc., 1932.

The Architecture of Old Kentucky. Frankfort, Kentucky: 1933.

The Colonial and Federal House: How to Build an Authentic Colonial House. Philadelphia: J.B. Lippincott Company, 1933.

Economic and Social Values of Good Architecture. Urbana: 1934.

Spanish Colonial Architecture in the United States. New York: J.J. Augustin, 1937.

Old Kentucky Architecture: Colonial, Federal, Greek Revival, Gothic. New York: William Helburn Inc., 1940.

History of Modern Architecture. Scranton: International Textbook Company, 1942.

Outlines of the History of Architecture, Revised. Champaign: Illini Union Bookstore, 1946.

Architecture of the Old Northwest Territory. Chicago: University of Chicago Press, 1950.

Architecture in Old Kentucky. Urbana: University of Illinois Press, 1953.

Miscellaneous Publications and Articles

In addition to the above books, Rexford Newcomb wrote numerous articles and book reviews published in various periodicals. Among these was an important series of articles on "The Architecture of the Spanish Renaissance in California", published in *The Western Architect* between 1919 and 1923. Most of his articles were published in *The Western Architect* and *The Architect*, and several appeared in *Architectural Forum*, *Architecture*, and *Construction Details.* A few were published independently, and *The Associated Tile Manufacturers* issued a number of his monographs on tile and tilework.

SELECTED BIBLIOGRAPHY OF PUBLICATIONS RELATING TO THE MEDITERRANEAN REVIVAL

Ames, Meriam, et al, eds. *Rancho Santa Fe: A California Village.* Rancho Santa Fe, California: The Rancho Santa Fe Historical Society, 1993.

Amicis, Edmondo de. *Spain and the Spaniards.* 2 vols. Philadelphia: Henry T. Coates & Co., 1895.

Andree, Herb, Noel Young and Wayne McCall. *Santa Barbara Architecture: From Spanish Colonial to Modern.* Santa Barbara, California: Capra Press, 1975.

Bailley, Vernon Howe. *Little Known Towns of Spain.* New York: William Helburn Inc., 1927.

Belloli, Jay, et al. *Wallace Neff 1895 - 1982: The Romance of Regional Architecture.* San Marino, California: The Huntington Library, 1989.

—. *Johnson, Kaufmann, Coate: Partners in the California Style.* Claremont, California: Scripps-Capra Press, 1992.

Bissell, Ervanna Bowen. *Glimpses of Santa Barbara and Montecito Gardens.* Santa Barbara, California: 1926.

Boston Architectural Club (Frederic V. Little, Executive Secretary). *The Book of the Boston Architectural Club for 1925: Spain.* Boston: Boston Architectural Club Inc., 1926.

Bottomley, William Lawrence. *Spanish Details.* New York: William Helburn Inc., 1924.

Byne, Arthur and Mildred Stapley. *Rejeria of the Spanish Renaissance.* New York: The Hispanic Society of America, 1914.

—. *Spanish Ironwork.* New York: The Hispanic Society of America, 1915.

—. *Decorated Wooden Ceilings in Spain.* Manual. New York: G.P. Putnam's Son's, 1920.

—. *Decorated Wooden Ceilings in Spain.* Portfolio of Plates. New York: G.P. Putnam's Son's, 1920.

—. *Spanish Gardens and Patios.* Philadelphia: J.B. Lippincott Company, 1924.

—. *Provincial Houses in Spain.* New York: William Helburn Inc., 1925.

—. *Spanish Interiors and Furniture.* 3 vols.. New York: William Helburn Inc., 1925.

—. *Majorcan Houses and Gardens.* New York: William Helburn Inc., 1928.

Byne, Mildred Stapley. *Forgotten Shrines of Spain.* Philadelphia: J.B. Lippincott Company, 1926.

Cheney, Sheldon. *The New World Architecture.* 1930. New York: Longmans, Green & Company, 1930.

Clark, Alson. "The 'Californian' Architecture of Gordon B. Kaufman." Review. *Society of Architectural Historians Southern California Chapter* Vol. 1, No. 3 (Summer, 1982): 2

Close, Bernard Wells, ed. *American Country House of Today.* New York: Architectural Book Publishing Co., 1922.

Conard, Rebecca and Christopher H. Nelson. *Santa Barbara: A Guide to El Pueblo Viejo.* Santa Barbara, California: The City of Santa Barbara, 1986.

Curl, Donald W. *Mizner's Florida.* New York: The Architectural History Foundation and the MIT Press, 1984.

Davis, Walter S., et al. *California Garden City Homes: A Book of Stock Plans.* Los Angeles: Garden City Company of California, 1915. Rev. ed. 1946 as *Ideal Homes in Garden Communities: A Book of House Plans.*

de Forest, Elizabeth. "Old Santa Barbara Gardens and How They Came to Be." *Pacific Horticulture* 38 (Winter 1977-78): 31-36.

Dobyns, Winifred Starr. *California Gardens.* New York: MacMillan Company, 1931.

Eberlein, Harold Donaldson. *Villas of Florence and Tuscany.* Philadelphia: J.B. Lippincott Company, 1922.

—. *Spanish Interiors.* New York: Architectural Book Publishing Co., 1925.

Edgell, G.H. *The American Architecture of To-Day.* New York: Charles Scribner's Sons, 1928.

Embury, Amyar II. *One Hundred Country Houses, Modern American Examples.* New York: Century Company, 1909.

Fatio, Alexandra, ed. *Maurice Fatio—Architect.* Palm Beach: privately published, 1992.

Feduchi, Luis. *Spanish Folk Architecture: The Northern Plateau.* Barcelona, Spain: Editorial Blume, 1974.

Fox, Helen Morgenthau. *Patio Gardens.* New York: MacMillan Company, 1929.

Garnett, Porter. *Stately Homes of California.* Boston: Little, Brown and Company, 1915.

Garrison, Richard and George Rustay. *Mexican Houses.* New York: Architectural Book Publishing Co., 1930.

Gebhard, David. *George Washington Smith, 1876-1930. The Spanish Colonial Revival In California.* Exhibition Catalogue. Santa Barbara, California: Art Gallery, University of California, Santa Barbara, 1964.

—. "The Spanish Colonial Revival in Southern California (1895 -1930)". *Journal of the Society of Architectural Historians* 26 (1967): 131-147.

— and Harriette Von Breton. *Architecture in California, 1868-1968.* Exhibition Catalogue. Santa Barbara, California: The Art Galleries, University of California, Santa Barbara, 1968.

— and Robert Winter. *A Guide to Architecture in Los Angeles and Southern California.* Santa Barbara and Salt Lake City: Peregrine Smith Inc., 1977.

—. *Santa Barbara-The Creation of a New Spain in America.* Exhibition Catalogue. Santa Barbara, California: University Art Museum, University of California, Santa Barbara, 1982.

—, David Bricker and Lauren Weiss Bricker. *A Catalogue of the Architectural Drawing Collection.* Santa Barbara, California: The University Art Museum, University of California, Santa Barbara, 1983.

—, ed. *Myron Hunt, 1868-1952: The Search for A Regional Architecture.* Santa Monica, California: Hennessey & Ingalls, Inc., 1984.

— and Sheila Lynds, eds. *An Arcadian Landscape: The California Gardens of A.E. Hanson 1920-1932.* Los Angeles: Hennessey & Ingalls, Inc. 1985.

—. "Founding Father: GWS". *Santa Barbara Magazine.* (July/August 1993).

Gleye, Paul. *The Architecture of Los Angeles.* Los Angeles: Rosebud-Knapp, 1981.

Grey, Elmer. "Southern California Architecture" and an article in *Southern California Home.* Privately published. Los Angeles: 1925.

Hannaford, Donald and Revel Edwards. *Spanish Colonial and Adobe Architecture of California, 1800-1850.* New York: Architectural Book Publishing Co., 1931.

Hewitt, Mark Alan. *The Architect & The American Country House 1890-1940.* New Haven: Yale University Press, 1990.

Hielscher, Kurt. *Picturesque Spain.* New York: Brentano's, 1922.

—. *Picturesque Italy.* New York: Brentano's, 1925.

Hooker, Marian Osgood, Katharine Hooker and Myron Hunt. *Farmhouses and Small Provincial Buildings in Southern Italy.* New York: Architectural Book Publishing Co., 1925.

Hunter, Paul Robinson and Walter L. Reichardt, eds. *Residential Architecture in Southern California.* Los Angeles: Southern California Chapter, AIA, 1939.

Jackson, Helen Hunt. *Ramona.* Boston: Roberts Brothers, 1884.

Johnston, Alva. *The Legendary Mizners.* New York: Farrar, Straus & Young, 1953.

Johnston, Shirley and Roberto Schezen. *Palm Beach Houses.* New York: Rizzoli, 1991.

Kaplan, Sam Hall. LA *Lost & Found: An Architectural History of Los Angeles.* New York: Crown Publishers Inc., 1987.

Keefe, Charles S., ed. *The American House.* New York: U.P.C. Book Company Inc., 1922.

Kirker, Harold. *California's Architectural Frontier.* 3rd ed. Santa Barbara and Salt Lake City: Gibbs M. Smith, 1986.

—. *Old Forms on a New Land, California Architecture in Perspective.* Colorado: Roberts Rinehart Publishers, 1991.

Kowalczyk, Georg and Gustavo Gili, ed. *Hierros Artisticos.* Barcelona, Spain: 1927.

Lane, Jonathan. "The Period House in the Nineteen-Twenties." *Journal of the Society of Architectural Historians* 20 (1961): 169-178.

Lockwood, Charles and Jeff Hyland. *The Estates of Beverly Hills.* Beverly Hills, California: Margrant Publishing Co., 1984.

Lowell, Guy. *More Small Italian Villas and Farmhouses.* Architectural Book Publishing Co., 1920.

—. *Smaller Italian Villas and Farmhouses.* New York: Architectural Book Publishing Co., 1922.

Mack, Gerstle and Thomas Gibson. *Architectural Details of Northern and Central Spain.* New York: William Helburn Inc., 1928.

—. *Architectural Details of Southern Spain.* New York: William Helburn Inc., 1928.

Major, Howard. *Palm Beach Villas.* Palm Beach: R.O. Davies Publishing Co., 1929.

Mayer, August L. *Alt-Spanien.* New York: Architectural Book Publishing Co., 1920.

—. *Architecture and Applied Arts of Old Spain.* New York: Brentano's, 1921.

McCoy, Esther. *Five California Architects.* New York: Reinhold Book Corporation, 1960.

McGrew, Patrick. *Landmarks of Los Angeles.* New York: Harry N. Abrams, Inc. Publishers, 1994.

Michael, A.C. *An Artist in Spain.* London: Hodder & Stoughton.

Mizner, Addison and Alice A. DeLamar. *Florida Architecture of Addison Mizner.* New York: William Helburn Inc., 1928. Reprinted by Dover Publications in 1992 with a new introduction by Donald W. Curl.

Mizner, Addison. *The Many Mizners.* New York: Sears Publishing Co., 1932.

Modern Homes: Their Design and Construction. Chicago: American Builder Publishing Corporation, 1931.

Moncanut, V. Casellas. *Arte y Decoracion en España.* 10 vols. Barcelona, Spain: J.M. Fabre, 1917-1924.

Moore, Charles, Gerald Allen and Donlyn Lyndon. *The Place of Houses.* New York: Holt, Rinehart and Winston, 1974.

Moore, Charles and Gerald Allen. *Dimensions.* New York: Architectural Record Books, 1976.

Moore, Charles, Peter Becker and Regula Campbell. *The City Observed: Los Angeles.* New York: Vintage Books, 1984.

Myrick, David F. *Montecito and Santa Barbara. Vol. 1: From Farms to Estates. Vol. II: The Days of the Great Estates.* Glendale, California: Trans-Anglo Books, 1988 and 1991.

Neff, Wallace. *Architecture of Southern California: A Selection of Photographs, Plans and Scale Details from the Work of Wallace Neff, FAIA.* Chicago: Rand McNally, 1964.

Neff, Wallace, Jr., ed., and Alson Clark. *Wallace Neff: Architect of California's Golden Age.* Santa Barbara, California: Capra Press, 1986.

Newcomb, Rexford. [See separate list of his publications].

Nichols, Rose Standish. *Spanish and Portuguese Gardens.* Boston: Houghton Mifflin Company, 1924.

Orr, Christina. *Addison Mizner: Architect of Dreams and Realities (1872-1933).* West Palm Beach: Davies Publishing Co., 1932.

Ovnick, Merry and Carol Monteverde. *Los Angeles: The End of the Rainbow.* Los Angeles: Balcony Press, 1994.

Padilla, Victoria. *Southern California Gardens.* Berkeley, California: University of California Press, 1961.

Patterson, Augusta Owen. *American Homes of To-Day: Their Architectural Style, Their Environment, Their Characteristics.* New York: MacMillan Co., 1924.

Polley, G.H. *Spanish Architecture and Ornament.* Boston: Geo. H. Polley & Co., 1889.

Polyzoides, Stefanos, Roger Sherwood, James Tice, Julius Shulman. *Courtyard Housing in Los Angeles.* Berkeley, California: University of California Press, 1982.

Power, Nancy Goslee. *The Gardens of California: Four Centuries of Design from Mission to Modern.* New York: Clarkson Potter Publishers, 1995.

Peixotto, Ernest. *Romantic California.* New York: Scribner's, 1917.

Prentice, A.N. *Renaissance Architecture and Ornament in Spain.* London: B.T. Batsford, 1888.

Requa, Richard S. *Architectural Details: Spain and the Mediterranean.* Cleveland, Ohio: J.H. Jansen, 1927.

—. *Old World Inspiration for American Architecture.* Los Angeles, California: The Monolith Portland Cement Company, 1929.

Sexton, R.W. *Spanish Influence on American Architecture and Decoration.* New York: Brentano's, 1927.

—. *American Country Houses of Today.* New York: Architectural Book Publishing Co., 1930.

Soule, Winsor. *Spanish Farm Houses and Minor Public Buildings.* New York: Architectural Book Publishing Co., 1924.

Staats, H. Philip. *California Architecture in Santa Barbara.* New Edition, 1990. Stamford, Connecticut: Architectural Book Publishing Co., 1929.

Stanton, J.E. *By Middle Seas.* Los Angeles: Gladding McBean & Co, 1927.

Starr, Kevin. *Americans and the California Dream, 1850-1915.* New York: Oxford University Press, 1973.

—. *Inventing the Dream: California Through the Progressive Era.* New York: Oxford University Press, 1985.

—. *Material Dreams: Southern California Through the 1920s.* New York: Oxford University Press, 1990.

Stern, Robert A.M. "The Anglo-American Suburb." *Architectural Digest* 1981: 4-12, 82.

Streatfield, David C. "The Evolution of the California Landscape." *Landscape Architecture.* Part 1. "Settling into Arcadia" (January 1976): 39-46.

—. "The Evolution of the California Landscape." *Landscape Architecture.* Part 2. "Arcadia Compromised" (March 1976): 117-26.

—. "The Evolution of the California Landscape." *Landscape Architecture.* Part 3. "The Great Promotions" (May 1977): 229-49.

—. "The Evolution of the California Landscape." *Landscape Architecture.* Part 4. "Suburbia at the Zenith" (September 1977): 417-24.

—. "The Garden at Casa del Herrero." *Antiques* 130 (August 1986): 287-88.

—. *California Gardens: Creating a New Eden.* New York: Abbeville Press Publishers, 1994.

Van Pelt, Garrett. *Old Architecture of Southern Mexico.* Cleveland, Ohio: J.H. Jansen, 1926.

Van Pelt, John V. *Masterpieces of Spanish Architecture: Romanesque and Allied Styles.* New York: Pencil Points Press, 1925.

Vogt, Elizabeth E. *Montecito: California's Garden Paradise.* Santa Barbara, California: MIP Publishing, 1993.

Waters, George. "Lotusland." *Pacific Horticulture* 44 (Spring 1983): 20-25.

Weitze, Karen J. *California's Mission Revival.* Los Angeles: Hennessey & Ingalls Inc., 1984.

Whitaker, Charles Harris, ed. *Bertram Grosvenor Goodhue: Architect and Master of Many Arts.* New York: Press of the American Institute of Architects, 1925.

Whittlesey, Austin. *The Minor Ecclesiastical, Domestic and Garden Architecture of Southern Spain.* New York: Architectural Book Publishing Co., 1917.

—. *The Renaissance Architecture of Central and Northern Spain.* New York: Architectural Book Publishing Co., 1920.

Winslow, Carleton Monroe, Bertram Grosvenor Goodhue and Clarence S. Stein . *The Architecture and the Gardens of the San Diego Exposition.* San Francisco: Paul Elder and Company, 1916.

Winslow, Carleton Monroe and Edward Fisher Brown, eds. *Small House Design.* 3rd. ed. Santa Barbara, California: Community Arts Association of Santa Barbara, California, 1924.

Yerbury, F.R. *Lesser Known Architecture of Spain.* New York: William Helburn Inc., 1925.

Yoch, James J. *Landscaping the American Dream: The Gardens and Film Sets of Florence Yoch: 1890-1972.* New York: Harry N. Abrams, 1989.

A number of the above books also contain bibliographies and/or footnotes referencing other sources, including many articles too numerous to list here, that were published in various professional and trade magazines and periodicals. Most of these articles were published during the period of the Mediterranean Revival. The following is a partial listing of periodicals in which they appeared, and some of their authors, in alphabetical order:

PERIODICALS:

The American Architect
The Architect
Architects and Builders Magazine
Architectural Forum
Architectural Record
The Architect and Engineer
Arts and Decoration
The Building Review
California Architect and Building News
California Arts and Architecture
California Southland
The Craftsman
House Beautiful
Journal of the American Institute of Architects
Land of Sunshine
Outwest
Pacific Coast Architect
Sunset
The Western Architect

AUTHORS:

David C. Allison
Harris Allen
George C. Baum
Arthur B. Benton
John Taylor Boyd, Jr.
Charles H. Cheney
Herbert D. Croly
Prentice Duell
Aymar Embury II
Giles Edgerton
Mary Pickford Fairbanks
H. Roy Kelly
A. Lawrence Kocher
Irving F. Morrow
Rexford Newcomb
Matlack Price
George H. Reed
M. Urmy Seares
Winsor Soule
G. Stanley Taylor
Charles F. Whittlesey

ACKNOWLEDGEMENTS

I am indebted to Sara Blackburn, Barry Cenower, Daniel Gregory, Allan Greenberg, Stephen Harby, and Mark Hewitt, who contributed valuable suggestions to the manuscript. Robert Chapel of the University of Illinois Library at Urbana-Champaign was most helpful in supplying biographical information on Newcomb. The late David Gebhard and his widow, Patricia Gebhard, have enlightened my studies over the years. Kurt Helfrich, the current director of the Architectural Drawings Collection of the University Art Museum, University of California, Santa Barbara, generously provided access to key architectural drawings. Brooke Gardner, my assistant, has patiently helped me throughout, especially with biographical research. Last but not least, I am grateful to my late grandmother, Angelica Bryce, and her daughter—my mother—Ariel Appleton, for the experience of knowing and loving a part of California history through their lives.

MEDITERRANEAN DOMESTIC ARCHITECTURE IN THE UNITED STATES

GARDEN OF MR. HENRY W. SCHULTZ, PASADENA, CALIFORNIA
WALLACE NEFF, ARCHITECT

MEDITERRANEAN DOMESTIC ARCHITECTURE IN THE UNITED STATES

By REXFORD NEWCOMB, A. I. A

1928

J. H. JANSEN, CLEVELAND, OHIO

PRINTED BY
THE ARTCRAFT PRINTING COMPANY
CLEVELAND, OHIO, U.S.A.

Barrio De Los Palmeras
Palm Beach Florida

ACKNOWLEDGMENT

IN the preparation of this volume the writer has had hearty co-operation of the many architects whose works are to be seen in these pages. To these men and to the WESTERN ARCHITECT, Inc., and THE ARCHITECT, for the use of some plates originally appearing in these journals the writer wishes to acknowledge his indebtedness.

REXFORD NEWCOMB

UNIVERSITY OF ILLINOIS
JULY 1, 1926

THE PUBLISHER THANKS MR. EDD A. RUGGLES OF THE CLEVELAND MUSEUM OF ART FOR ASSISTANCE IN THE TYPOGRAPHY OF THE BOOK

LIST OF ILLUSTRATIONS

MEDITERRANEAN DOMESTIC ARCHITECTURE IN THE UNITED STATES

By REXFORD NEWCOMB, A. I. A.

HOSE of us who gained our notions of American history from the typical grammar-school textbook of a third of a century ago know really very little concerning the peopling of our country outside that narrow area comprising the original thirteen states. That Florida, the Gulf Coast, Louisiana and the lower Mississippi Valley, to say nothing of Texas, New Mexico, Arizona, California and parts of Nevada, Utah and Colorado, were at one time parts of the vast world-flung domain of the Spanish kings is not well known or, if known, little remembered. To all this vast area architectural forms of Spanish origin or of related styles appear wonderfully adapted and within recent years have been sought out as inspiration by the more thoughtful practitioners in these and other states. This type of architecture in every way so expressive of the setting has, particularly in California and Florida, been so well adapted to modern American living conditions that it has well-nigh become the universal vernacular. Thus has California, and recently Florida, capitalized upon her history, romance and lore with the result that her architecture speaks more eloquently of her glorious present and colorful past than does any other phase of her artistic expression. What California has done, what Florida, Texas, Arizona and New Mexico are doing, a well informed and artistically inclined profession may do for other areas of our country.

The threads that weave themselves into that architectural fabric which we call "Spanish" go back in history a good many centuries. Based assuredly upon the round-arched, rhythmic forms of Roman Spain, this expression, as it came down through history, received the colorful Oriental threads of the North African Moor, the staunch monk's-cloth of the Burgundian Cluniacs, reflected in tapestried picture the curved gables and pierced belfries of Holland and the delicate, decorative, Gothic lacework of France and Germany and finished with the broad golden fringe of the Italian Renaissance.

This wonderfully varied warp and woof, drawn from so many sources, received in Spain a color and spirit that indelibly stamped it with that quality that we have for centuries now called "Spanish." Imported into the New World with the coming of the *Hidalgos* to our shores, this work of old Spain was modified in Mexico by the influence of the Aztecs and other splendid barbaric peoples, giving us a style far more varied than it had been in the home-land. Especially was this true as regards the use of colorful ceramic tiles upon *fachadas,* vaults and domes. Radiating northward and meeting special conditions in each of our American states to which it spread, this age-old Spanish-Mexican style was in each situation modified to give us the varied local expressions above mentioned. Thus our Spanish-Colonial, because of its peculiar parentage, its wide travels and its ranging climatic exposure, presents a variety of characteristics the like of which perhaps no other modern style embraces.

Most architects are familiar with the career in our country of that other sun-begotten style—the Italian Renaissance—so much used in the United States since the Exposition of 1893. Employed first for monumental architecture and eventually as the vernacular for large residential work, particularly country residences, it has given us little in the way of smaller residential types, though in recent years there has been a tendency in this direction. But the Italians did not conquer nor settle any part of our domain and consequently the Italian has always appeared in the guise of a borrowed style, however beautifully it has, in some cases, been adapted to American conditions. Therefore it has had little part in forming the great body of our residential architecture.

Called upon to do "Spanish" work, many of our men versed in the Italian, unconsciously allowed the Italian to modify their less well understood Spanish forms so that something that was neither Spanish nor Italian resulted. But this was only natural and, indeed, not so ridiculous as it might at first seem. As a matter of fact, we are neither Spaniards nor Italians and the work in California, Florida, Arizona, or Texas would contribute little were it simply archaeological parrot-phrases of these Old World works. By this curious accident of artistic history in our own land, again the Italian meets the Spanish as it did under the influence of the Renaissance in Old Spain.

Recognizing the affinities between the Spanish, Italian and, indeed, even North African work, an affinity most certainly testified to by the varying elements of our own Spanish Colonial, there has been a tendency further to mix the elements of these styles and many of our architects, seeking a wider inspiration and virtuosity of expression than the various types of our Spanish-Colonial afford, go back to the parent styles which, in times gone by, have so eloquently contributed to this cosmopolitan expression. Thus the fine old examples of Spain, of Italy, of North Africa, and in fact of most of the Mediterranean countries are being sought out as inspiration for modern work. And this is as it should be for, as there is much that the desert architecture of North Africa may contribute to the desert architecture of our arid Southwest, so in each country there are many situations that artistically parallel American conditions. Florida, for instance, while she is Hispanic in history and geographical associations, is in some of her aspects distinctly Italian—Venetian Italian. Thus one is not surprised to see along some lagoon in Florida a house, generally Spanish in feeling, with a doorway that recalls Murano and a balcony that recalls the "*Mistress of the Adriatic*" herself. Spanish, Italian, Moorish, Byzantine—Mediterranean types generally—instead of being kept archaeologically segregated, are under this orchestral process merged, as were those golden threads of long ago, into a new sun-loving style which, while eminently American in its plan and utilities, is never-the-less distinctly Mediterranean in its origins and spirit.

In view of this great variety of expression it is difficult to catalog the characteristics of this new "Mediterranean" architecture. except in a very broad and general way. Like domestic architecture in the Mediterranean area from the days of the Greek *Megaron* and Roman *Atrium* down, these houses find themselves disposed around an open courtyard or "*patio*," one or more sides of which may be lined with arcades of weights varying from the heavy arch-and-pier types of rural Spain to the delicate loggias of the Italian Renaissance. In some of our late smaller types two sides of the house only flank this court, the remaining sides being closed by high stucco-covered walls.

At the centre of this *patio*, which may be simply gravelled, flagged, or brick-paved, there is usually a fountain. This may be anything from a simple low bird-bath to an octagonal, tile-plated basin or an Italian terraced fountain. In any case potted geraniums and other floral varieties contribute their note of joyous color. Plantings of banana, oleander and other semi-tropical or tropical plants make green splotches against the broad areas of delicately tinted stucco. These features with the splash of vari-colored awnings, the sharp staccato notes of the wooden or wrought-iron grilles, heavy wooden shutters of brilliant colors, deep revealed windows, door heads of the utmost variety of shapes, the concentration of elaborate ornament around openings—especially around doors and important windows—these and a delightful regard for landscaped effects, go to make up the salient features of this delightful style that in the sunnier, more favored areas of our country will become increasingly popular as time goes on.

Nor must one be misled into believing that Mediterranean types of similar form are adaptable to the whole of the above named extensive areas, for this is not true. California, with its wide range of climate, its mission history, its peculiar coast situation and its variety of flora, will accept forms that would not appear at all well in New Mexico or Texas. Here the simplest of forms are enhanced by a wonderfully clear and vibrant atmosphere and the deep purple shadows induced by a vivid white sunshine, thus making unnecessary the elaborate forms and detail called for by less brilliantly lighted landscapes. This fundamental simplicity of the architectural forms makes it possible to develop a delightfully varied domestic architecture with the fewest of expedients. In this respect California has an artistic handicap over her less-favored neighbors, and Californian architects have given us most delightful examples expressed with a restraint that is as frugal, straightforward, honest and craftsmanlike as the old mission houses, the simple forms which to this day make such stunning pictures under California's white sun.

The forms of Arizona, on the other hand, are allied more closely to the Sonoran types of northern Mexico and partake of a large amount of "desert" feeling. Here the early Spanish domestic types, unlike the Californian work which presents widely projecting roofs covered with vari-colored, hand-made Spanish tiles, were flat roofed, and thus contrast with the churches which show low domes or tunnel vaults, features which, as a matter of fact, figure very little in the perspective. Again, the houses contrast markedly with the churches in that they are eminently plain in detail while the churches, like San Xavier del Bac, a fine old Franciscan structure near

Tucson, present *fachadas* more or less elaborately modelled and "polychromed." The "desert" quality of many Arizona situations would prompt the architect to seek in Algerian, Moroccan or other desert types inspiration for his work.

At Santa Fé and in New Mexico generally we find an entirely different architectural expression. Here the Spanish *Conquistadors* found a sedentary Indian population who had already developed an expressive native architecture. This many-terraced type, fine examples of which are still to be seen at Taos, Laguna, San Ildefonso and other places, generally passes under the name "*pueblo*." When the Spaniards employed these Indians to build structures, with European plans and utilities, of the materials and upon the lines of the native work, there resulted a new type, half-Spanish, half-Indian, the like of which has been nowhere else developed.

This type, often spoken of as the work of "the Santa Fé school," and eminently expressive of the ethnic backgrounds and geological formation of New Mexico, has been much used at Albuquerque, Santa Fé and elsewhere in the state with the result that the manner now embraces, in addition to residential types, structures as varied as churches and theatres, hospitals, museums and schools, the University of New Mexico, warehouses, power-houses, business buildings and clubs. Thus, this region has capitalized upon its heritage with such satisfactory results, that it is unlikely that the recent "Mediterranean" vogue will materially affect the career of architecture in this section.

Texas and the Gulf Coast present climates ranging from the humid and warm to the dry, semi-desert; thus here a great variety of expression may be expected. In certain of the plains areas "desert" types are very appropriate, while along the Gulf Coast and in the better watered and warmer sections architectural forms reflective of the semi-tropics are natural and appropriate.

When Florida became American in 1821 most of the old Spanish families remained to give to this old outpost of Spain the Hispanic flavor it still retains to this day. Although Florida has had champions for her beauties and resources from the days of Ponce de Leon on, relatively few Americans learned to enjoy her charms until Henry M. Flagler constructed the Florida East Coast Railway from Saint Augustine southward along the coast and over the Keys to Key West. The construction of this line made accessible many places that heretofore had been approachable only by water. The building by Messrs. Carrere and Hastings of the great hotels at Jacksonville and St. Augustine, and by others at Palm Beach and Miami, completed the facilities for tourist travel initiated by the railroad and the growth of the Florida winter resorts began. This development, beginning in the middle nineties, has continued until this time, each year seeing an increased patronage at these palatial hostelries. The last few years especially have seen an unprecedented movement toward Florida and the development of relatively large towns. This movement will result, without doubt, in an ever increasing resident population with the architectural development that a permanent population demands.

In a land so tropical as is the peninsula, where all sorts of citrus trees—oranges, lemons, grape fruit—and the jessamine, oleander, almond, banana, cork and coconut palm flourish, a sunny Mediterranean type of architecture is perfectly appropriate and to be expected. Therefore, basing their work securely upon the florid types of the Spanish Renaissance, a style suggested alike by historic background and material surroundings, the architects have modified this by suggestions from the Italian, the Moorish of Spain and North Africa, the Mexican Colonial and Venetian Gothic. All these and many other sunny types are drawn upon, as occasion dictates, to make the present day architecture catholic in range and yet as tropical in spirit as its most ardent champions would wish it. That much of the work, especially that to be found in some of the "developments" and "sub-divisions," is little less than theatrical stage-sets, is to be expected in a country where towns grow up as if by magic, yet there is much work—a very large amount in fact—that rings true to the high test demanded of good architecture in any place or clime.

The glistening rough-cast stucco walls, the glint of red tile roofs, the splash of brilliantly colored awnings, a liberal use of colorful decorative tiles and wrought-iron combine to give us a Mediterranean architectural expression that looks remarkably well and is eminently appropriate to a luxuriant setting of palm trees and oleander. Like sunny villas upon some enchanted island in a summer sea, these residences make the most pleasant retreats from our northern winter cold. To be sure, often the patios of these houses are, in the lazy, sultry days of summer, given over to scarlet flamingoes who fly up squalling at the intrusion of a visitor, but as winter retreats they are delights and stand as interesting examples of this new Mediterranean movement.

Thus the many divisions of this great sunny domain of our country present a variety of characteristics that must be taken into consideration by the architect who proposes to erect work in the Mediterranean manner. But, by relying upon the early local expression in each community and by the judicious selection of forms from the varied parent styles of Spain, Mexico, Italy or North Africa the architect of our time may find a grammar sufficiently broad to mirror every phase of life as it expresses itself in these various states.

ILLUSTRATIONS

Barrio De Los Palmeras
Palm Beach Florida
Architects

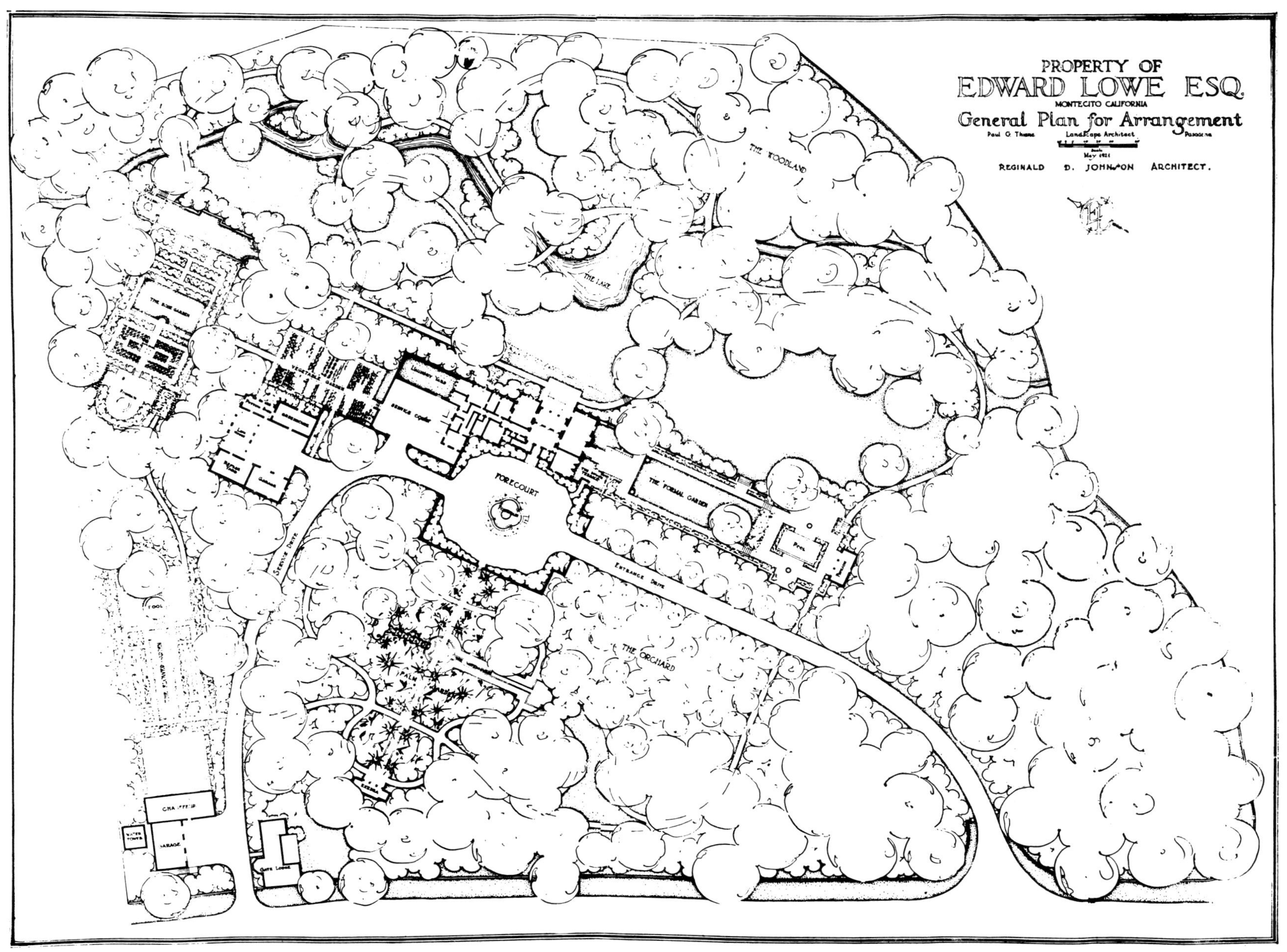

PLAN OF ESTATE ESTATE OF MR. EDWARD LOWE, MONTECITO, CALIFORNIA
REGINALD D. JOHNSON, ARCHITECT; PAUL G. THIENE, LANDSCAPE ARCHITECT

THE HOUSE, ENTRANCE DETAIL

THE HOUSE, FORECOURT DETAIL

ESTATE OF MR. EDWARD LOWE, MONTECITO, CALIFORNIA

REGINALD D. JOHNSON, ARCHITECT

THE HOUSE, FORECOURT FACADE ESTATE OF MR. EDWARD LOWE, MONTECITO, CALIFORNIA
REGINALD D. JOHNSON, ARCHITECT

THE PAVILION, DETAIL

THE HOUSE, LIVING ROOM FIREPLACE

ESTATE OF MR. EDWARD LOWE, MONTECITO, CALIFORNIA

REGINALD D. JOHNSON, ARCHITECT

THE GARDENS FROM THE PAVILION

ESTATE OF MR. EDWARD LOWE, MONTECITO, CALIFORNIA

REGINALD D. JOHNSON, ARCHITECT

ENTRANCE COURT

FACADE DETAIL

DOORWAY

ESTATE OF MR. J. P. JEFFERSON, MONTECITO, CALIFORNIA

REGINALD D. JOHNSON, ARCHITECT; PAUL G. THIENE, LANDSCAPE ARCHITECT

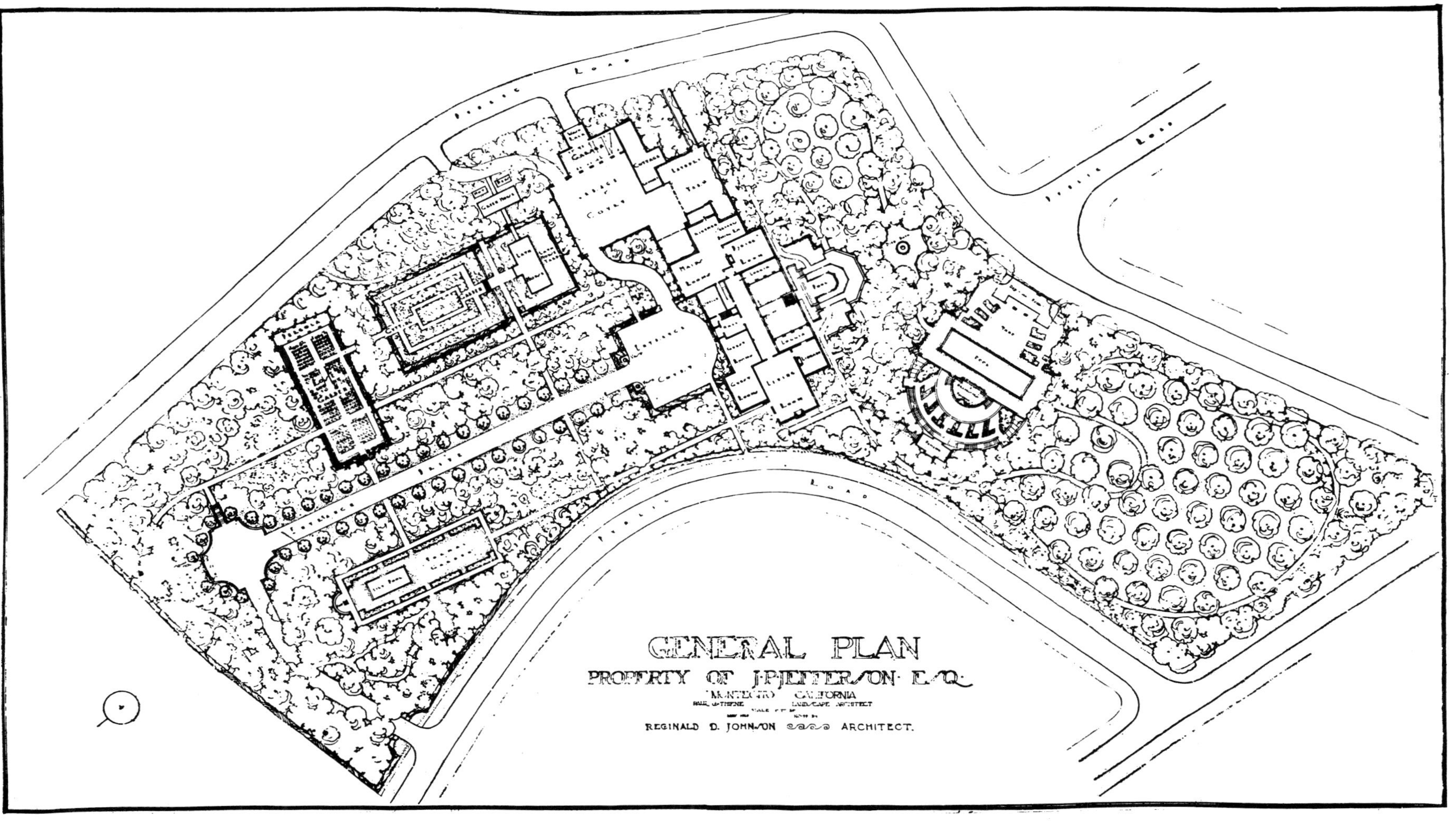

PLAN ESTATE OF MR. J. P. JEFFERSON, MONTECITO, CALIFORNIA

REGINALD D. JOHNSON, ARCHITECT; PAUL G. THIENE, LANDSCAPE ARCHITECT

GARDEN FACADE AND POOL, BACCHANTE BY McMONNIES

ESTATE OF MR. J. P. JEFFERSON, MONTECITO, CALIFORNIA

REGINALD D. JOHNSON, ARCHITECT; PAUL G. THIENE, LANDSCAPE ARCHITECT

HOUSE, HALL ESTATE OF MR. J. P. JEFFERSON, MONTECITO, CALIFORNIA
REGINALD D. JOHNSON, ARCHITECT; PAUL G. THIENE, LANDSCAPE ARCHITECT

HOUSE, ENTRANCE HALL

GARDEN, POOL AND PERGOLA

ESTATE OF MR. J. P. JEFFERSON, MONTECITO, CALIFORNIA

REGINALD D. JOHNSON, ARCHITECT; PAUL G. THIENE, LANDSCAPE ARCHITECT

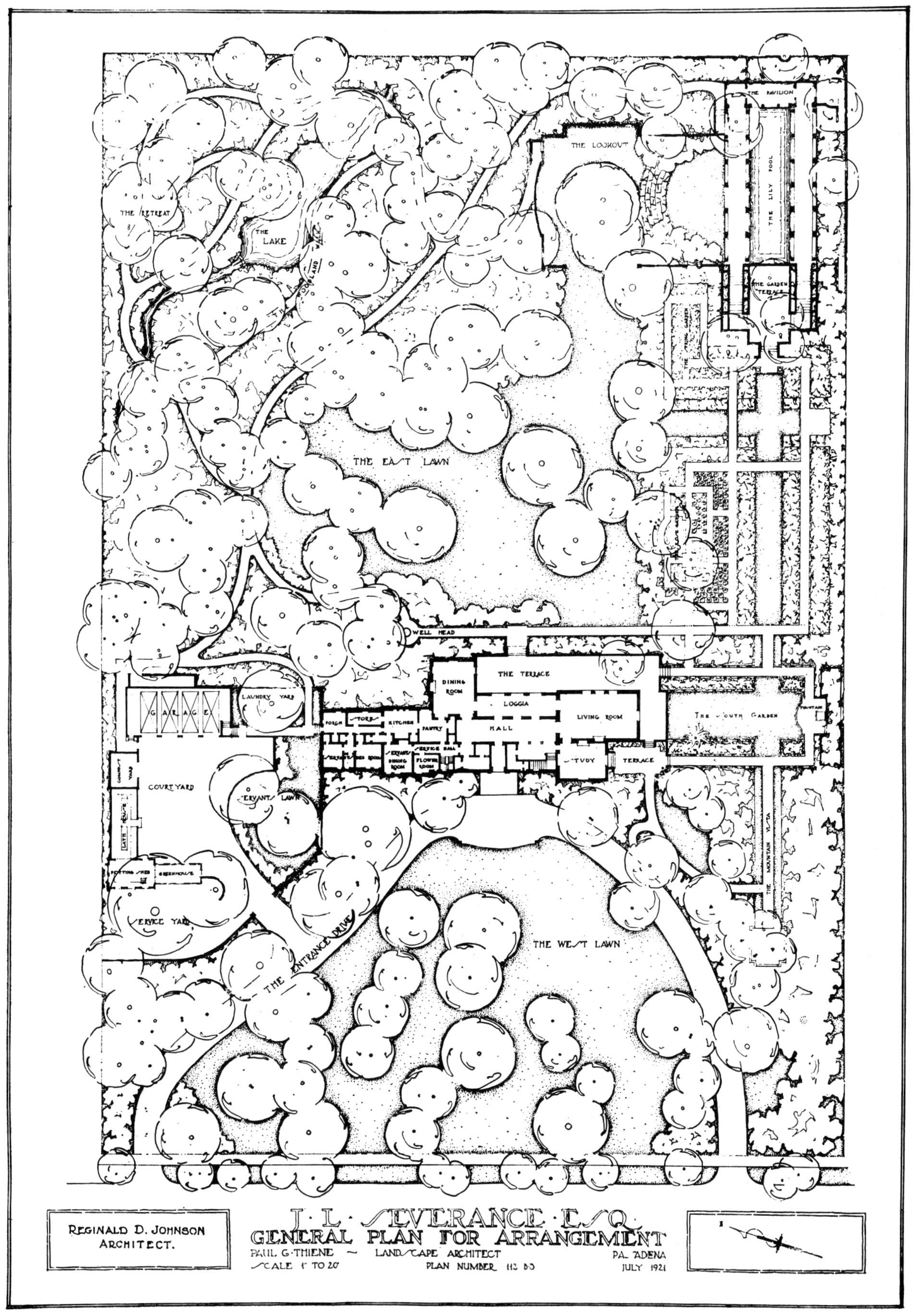

PLAN OF ESTATE ESTATE OF MR. J. L. SEVERANCE, PASADENA, CALIFORNIA

REGINALD D. JOHNSON, ARCHITECT

FORMAL POOL

ESTATE OF MR. J. L. SEVERANCE, PASADENA, CALIFORNIA

REGINALD D. JOHNSON, ARCHITECT; PAUL G. THIENE, LANDSCAPE ARCHITECT

POOL FROM GARDEN PAVILION

ESTATE OF MR. J. L. SEVERANCE, PASADENA, CALIFORNIA

REGINALD D. JOHNSON, ARCHITECT; PAUL G. THIENE, LANDSCAPE ARCHITECT

INTERIOR OF GARDEN PAVILION

STEPS IN GARDEN

ESTATE OF MR. J. L. SEVERANCE, PASADENA, CALIFORNIA

REGINALD D. JOHNSON, ARCHITECT; PAUL G. THIENE, LANDSCAPE ARCHITECT

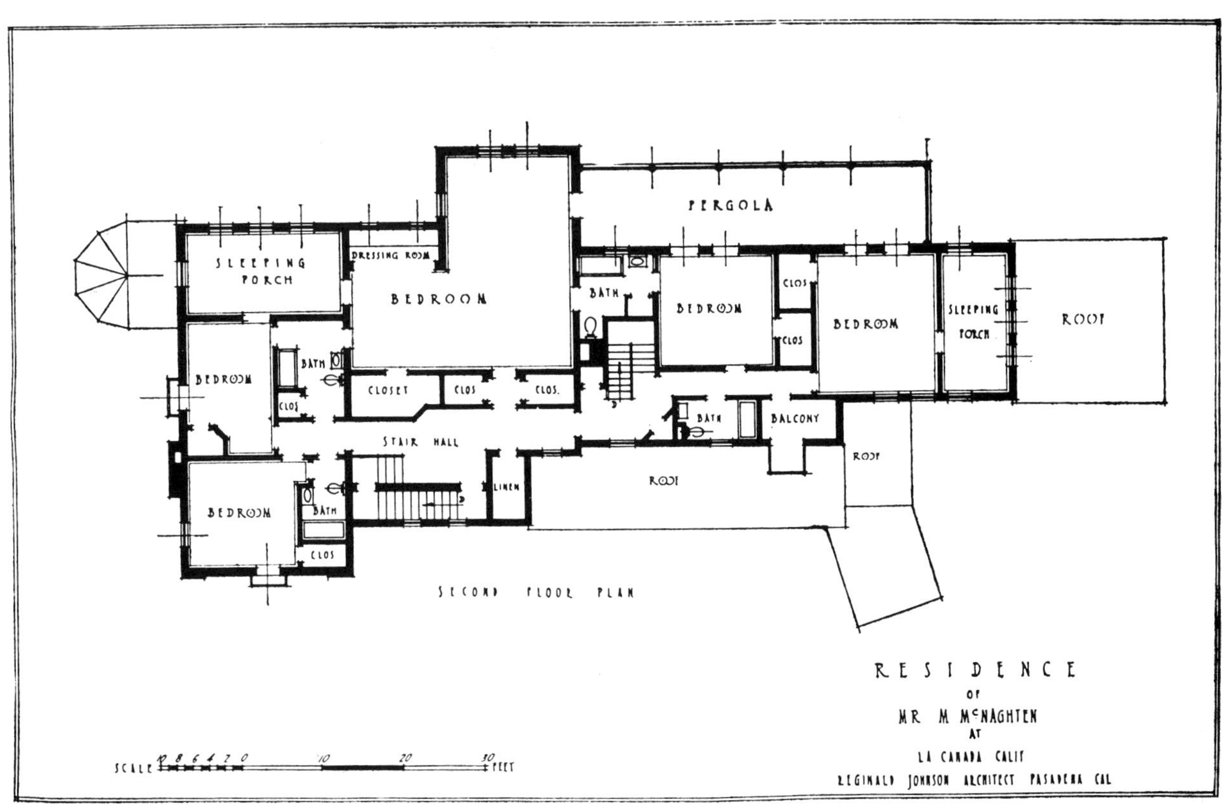

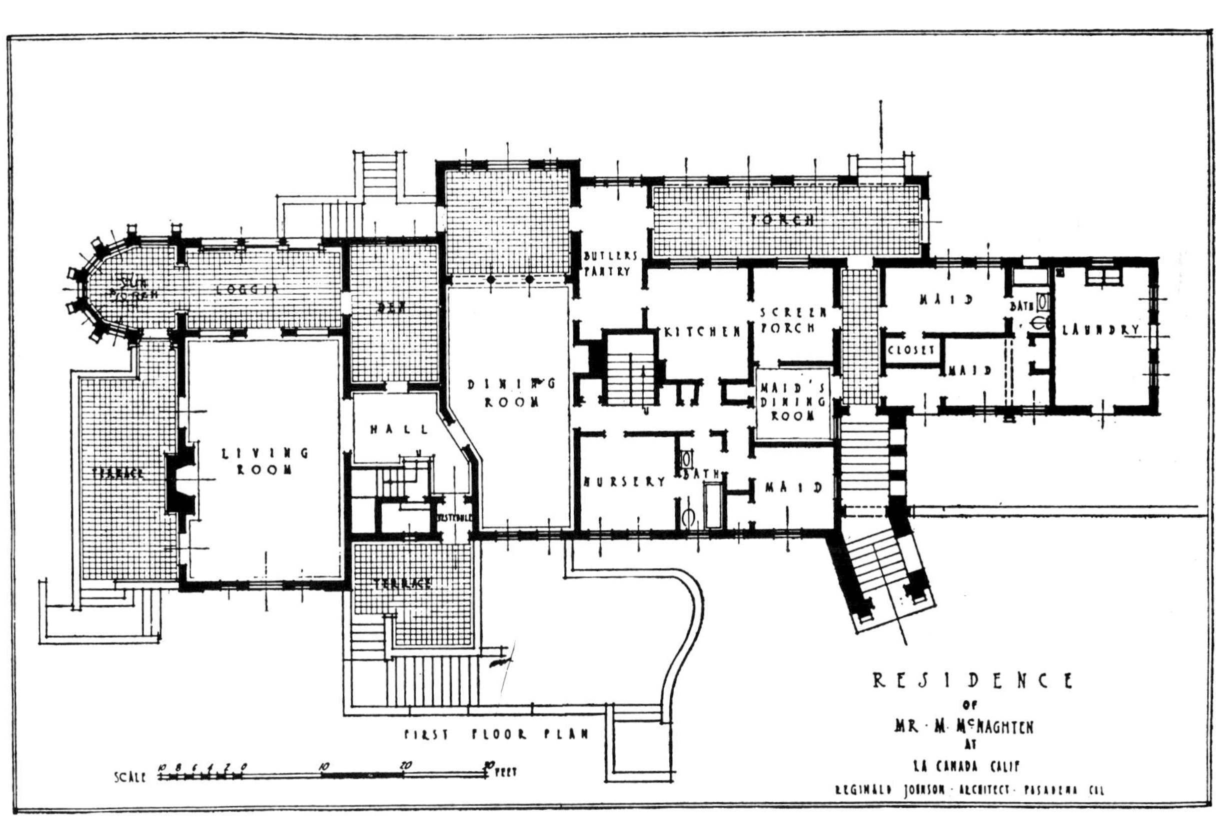

RESIDENCE FOR MR. MALCOLM McNAUGHTON, LA CAÑADA, CALIFORNIA

REGINALD D. JOHNSON, ARCHITECT

VIEWS OF HOUSE

RESIDENCE FOR MR. MALCOLM McNAUGHTON, LA CAÑADA, CALIFORNIA

REGINALD D. JOHNSON, ARCHITECT

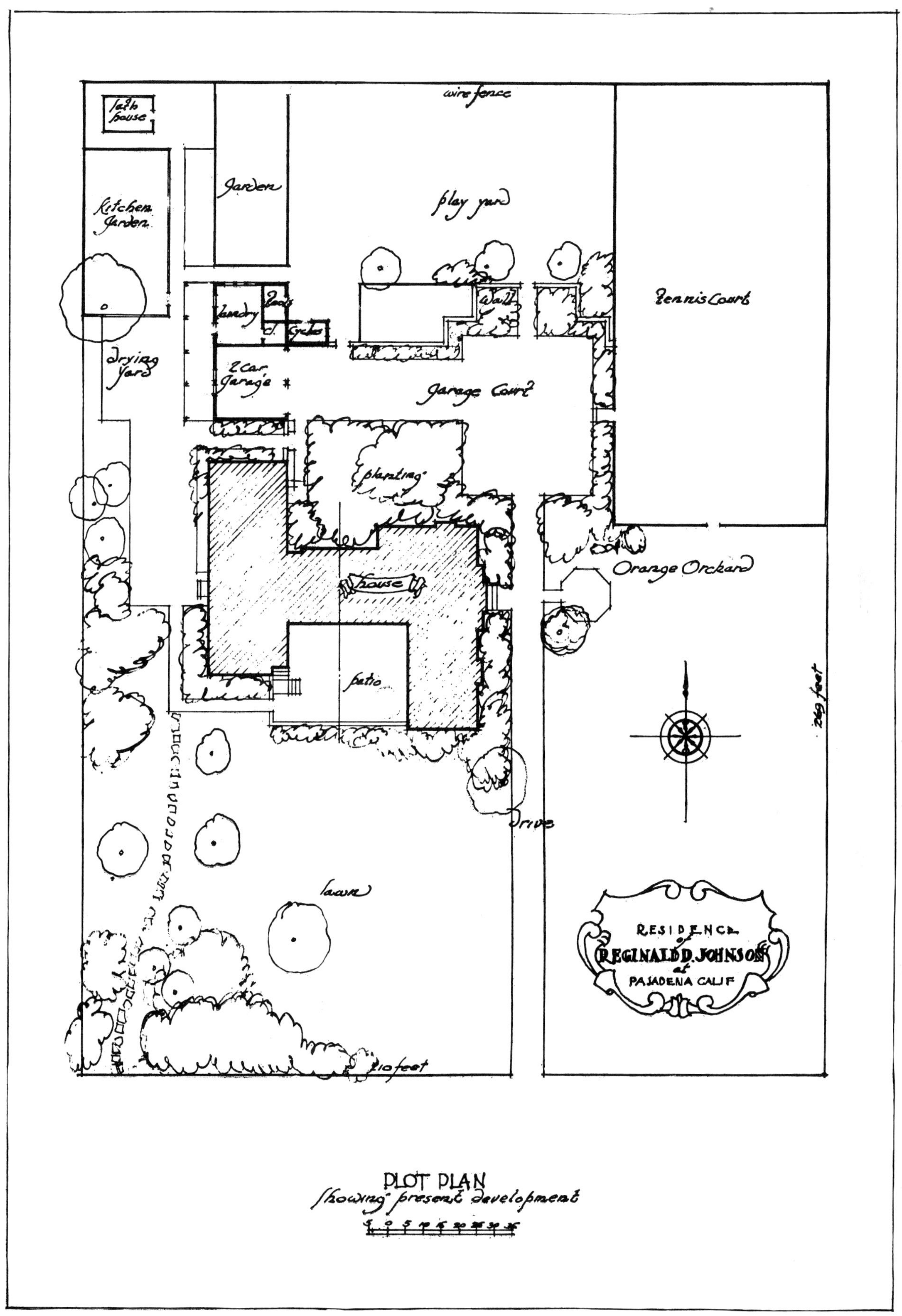

PLOT PLAN

RESIDENCE FOR MR. REGINALD D. JOHNSON, PASADENA, CALIFORNIA

REGINALD D. JOHNSON, ARCHITECT

GENERAL VIEW RESIDENCE FOR MR. REGINALD D. JOHNSON, PASADENA, CALIFORNIA

REGINALD D. JOHNSON, ARCHITECT

PATIO DETAIL

DOORWAY

RESIDENCE FOR MR. REGINALD D. JOHNSON, PASADENA, CALIFORNIA

REGINALD D. JOHNSON, ARCHITECT

GENERAL VIEW RESIDENCE FOR MR. W. H. PETERS, PASADENA, CALIFORNIA
MARSTON, VAN PELT & MAYBURY, ARCHITECTS

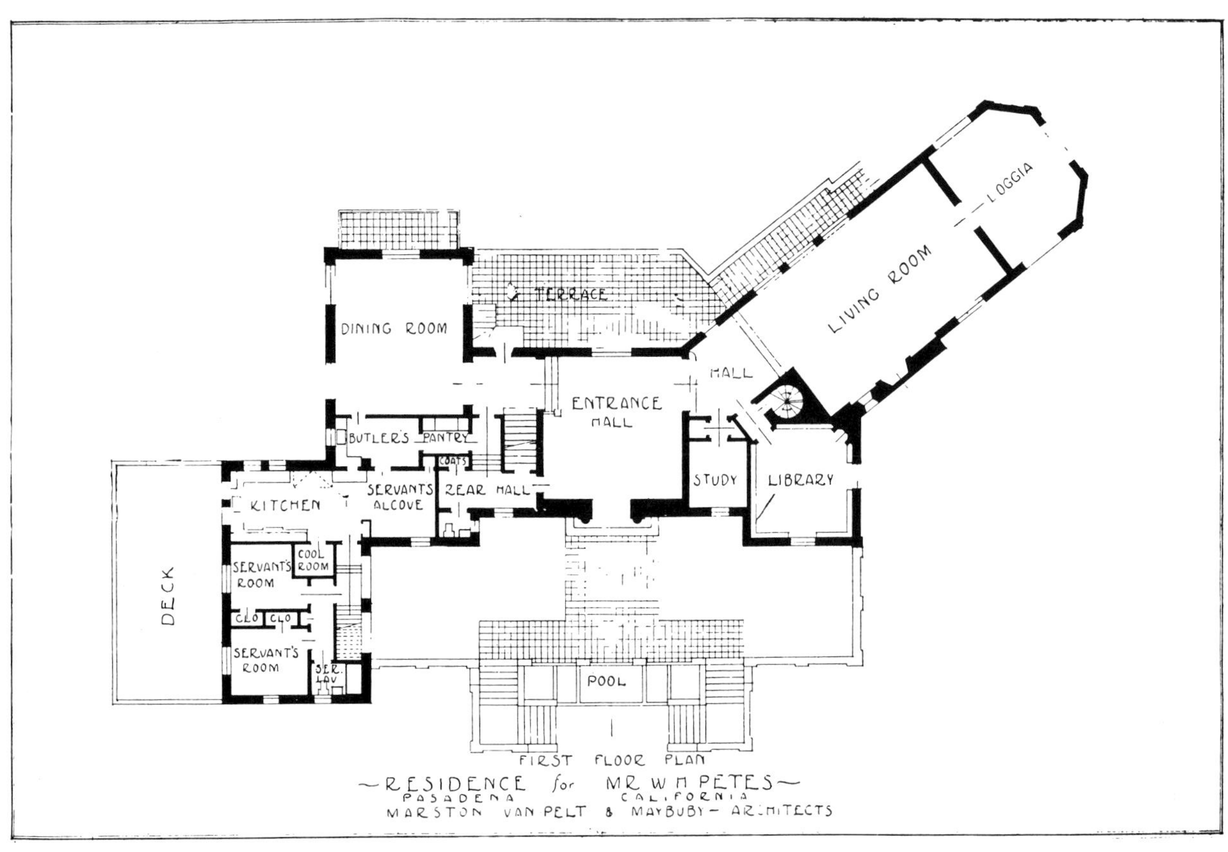

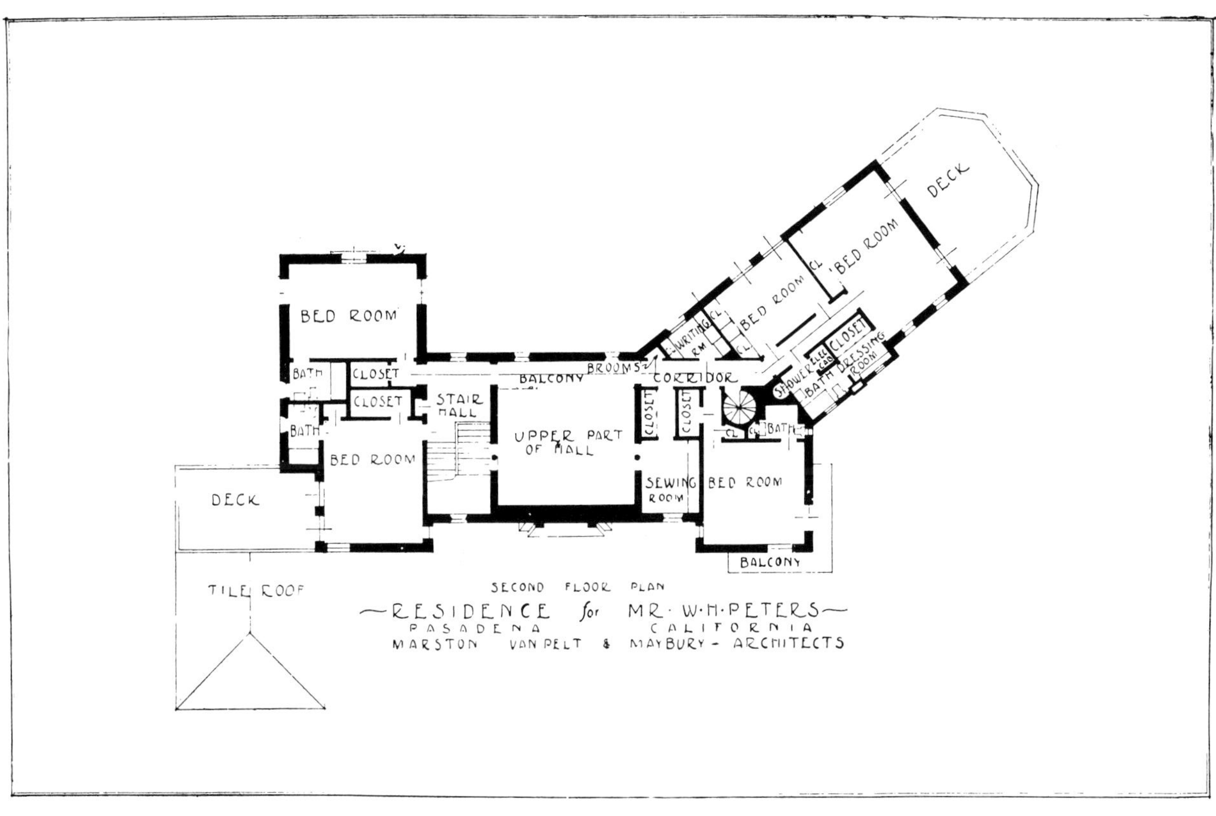

RESIDENCE FOR MR. W. H. PETERS, PASADENA, CALIFORNIA

MARSTON, VAN PELT & MAYBURY, ARCHITECTS

MAIN ENTRANCE, BALCONY DETAIL

ENTRANCE DETAIL

RESIDENCE FOR MR. W. H. PETERS, PASADENA, CALIFORNIA

MARSTON, VAN PELT & MAYBURY, ARCHITECTS

TERRACE

LOGGIA

RESIDENCE FOR MR. W. H. PETERS, PASADENA, CALIFORNIA

MARSTON, VAN PELT & MAYBURY, ARCHITECTS

THE GARDEN, POOL AND WALK

RESIDENCE FOR MR. W. H. PETERS, PASADENA, CALIFORNIA

MARSTON, VAN PELT & MAYBURY, ARCHITECTS

FOUNTAIN IN THE GARDEN FROM THE TERRACE

THE GARDEN, COLORADO STREET BRIDGE FROM THE PERGOLA

RESIDENCE FOR MR. W. H. PETERS, PASADENA, CALIFORNIA

MARSTON, VAN PELT & MAYBURY, ARCHITECTS

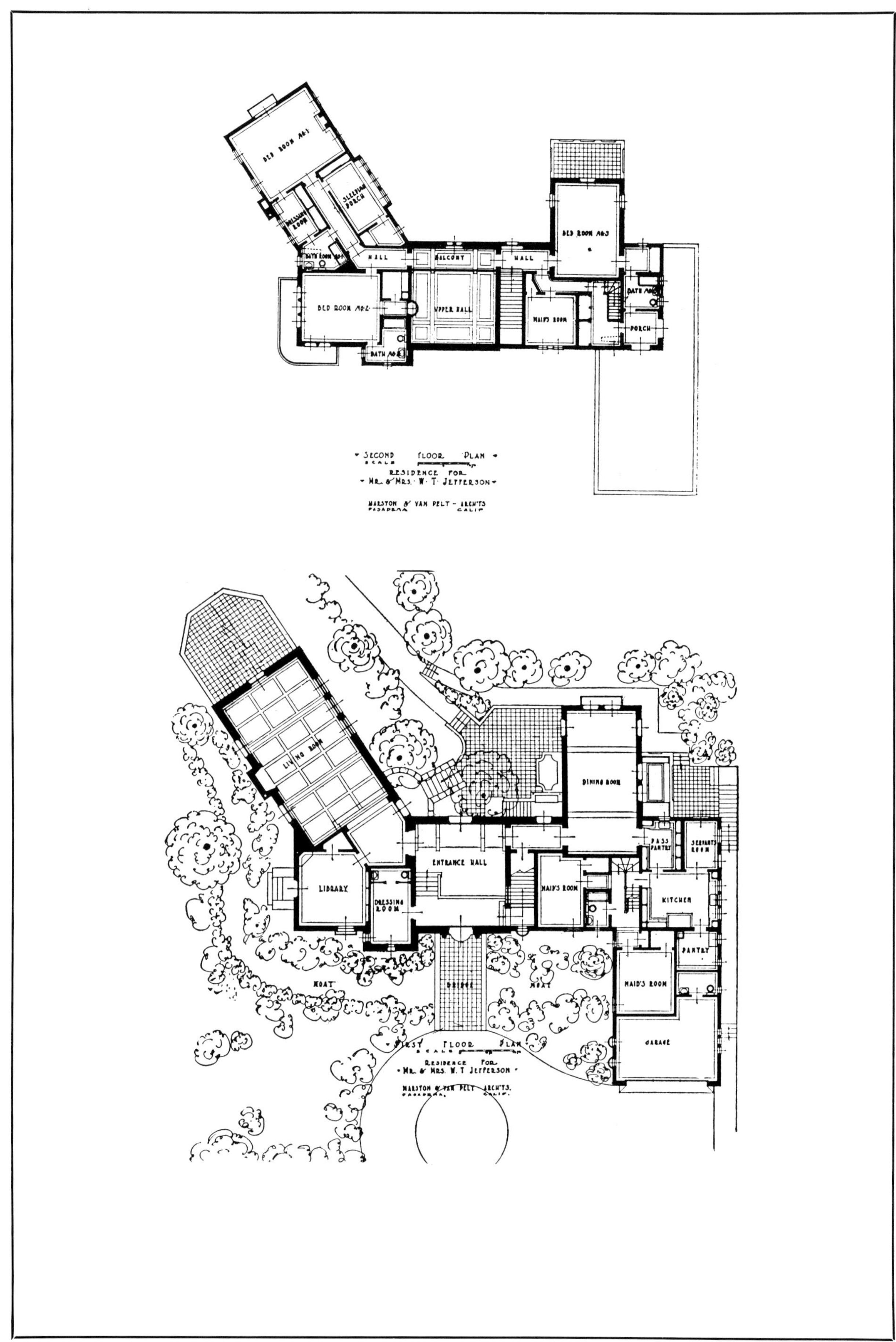

RESIDENCE FOR MR. W. J. JEFFERSON, PASADENA, CALIFORNIA

MARSTON, VAN PELT & MAYBURY, ARCHITECTS

ENTRANCE FRONT

DOORWAY

DOOR DETAIL

RESIDENCE FOR MR. W. J. JEFFERSON, PASADENA, CALIFORNIA

MARSTON, VAN PELT & MAYBURY, ARCHITECTS

ENTRANCE FRONT FROM GATE

BALCONY OVERLOOKING THE GARDEN

DETAIL

GARDEN ENTRANCE

RESIDENCE FOR MR. W. J. JEFFERSON, PASADENA, CALIFORNIA

MARSTON, VAN PELT & MAYBURY, ARCHITECTS

ENTRANCE HALL

ENTRANCE HALL

ENTRANCE TO LIVING ROOM

LIVING ROOM

RESIDENCE FOR MR. W. J. JEFFERSON, PASADENA, CALIFORNIA

MARSTON, VAN PELT & MAYBURY, ARCHITECTS

FACADE FROM ENTRANCE COURT

COURT FACADE

RESIDENCE FOR MR. JOHN HENRY MEYER, PASADENA, CALIFORNIA

MARSTON, VAN PELT & MAYBURY, ARCHITECTS

GARDEN FACADE

DETAIL

RESIDENCE FOR MR. JOHN HENRY MEYER, PASADENA, CALIFORNIA

MARSTON, VAN PELT & MAYBURY, ARCHITECTS

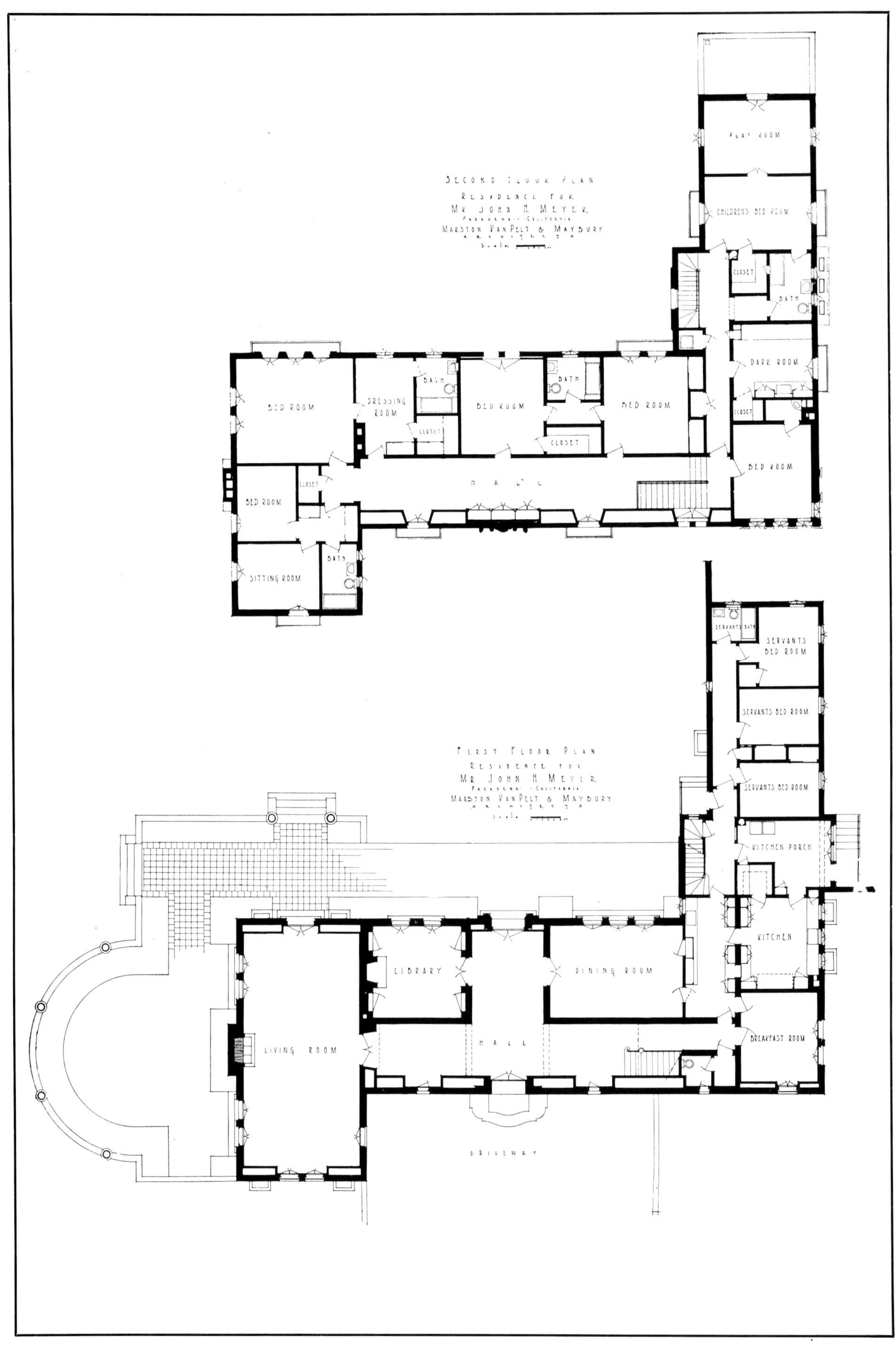

PLANS

RESIDENCE FOR MR. JOHN HENRY MEYER, PASADENA, CALIFORNIA

MARSTON, VAN PELT & MAYBURY, ARCHITECTS

GARDEN ENTRANCE

MAIN ENTRANCE

RESIDENCE FOR MR. JOHN HENRY MEYER, PASADENA, CALIFORNIA

MARSTON, VAN PELT & MAYBURY, ARCHITECTS

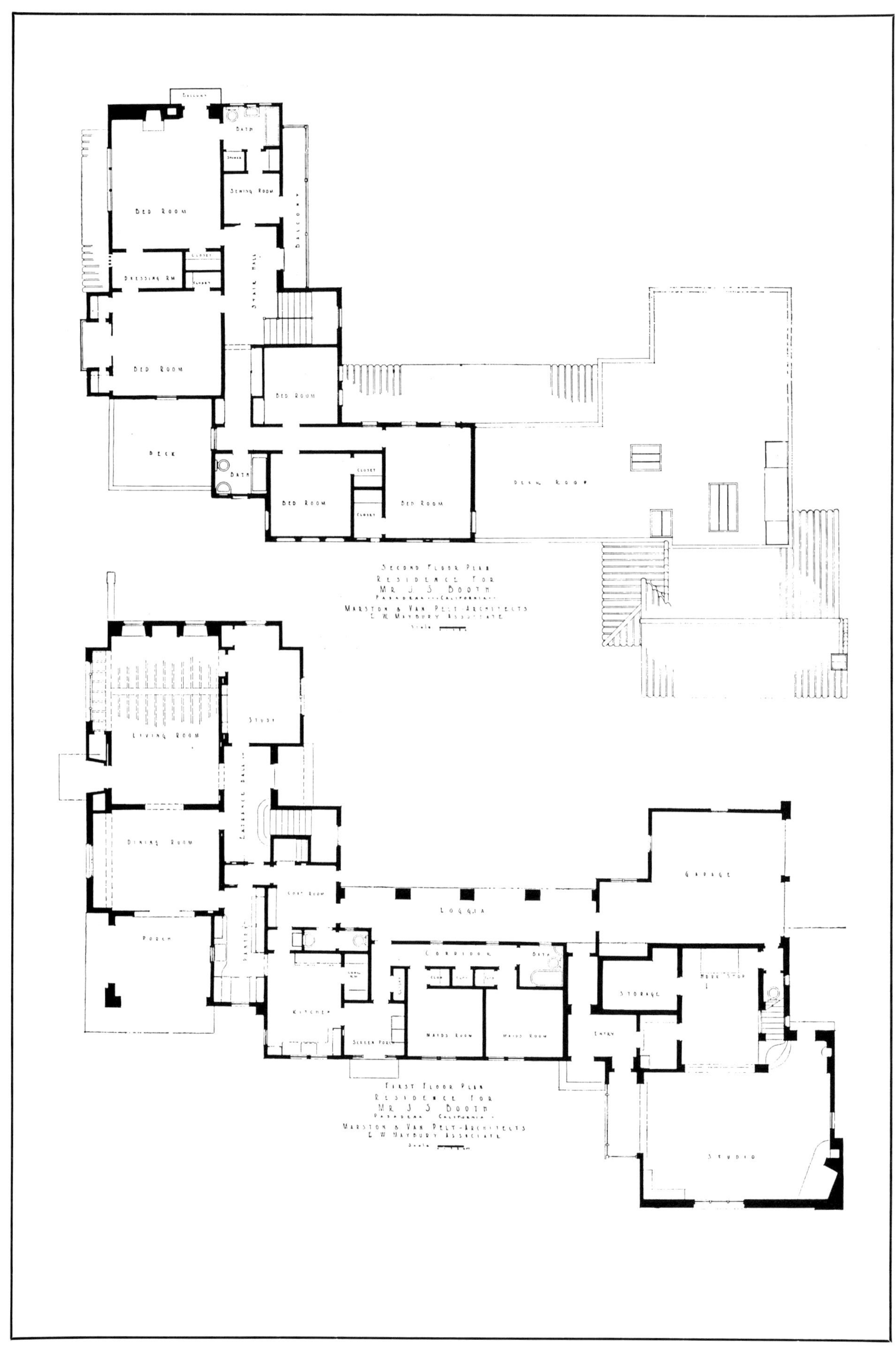

PLANS

RESIDENCE FOR MR. JAMES SCRIPPS-BOOTH, LINDA VISTA, CALIFORNIA

MARSTON, VAN PELT & MAYBURY, ARCHITECTS

GENERAL VIEW   RESIDENCE FOR MR. JAMES SCRIPPS-BOOTH, LINDA VISTA, CALIFORNIA
MARSTON, VAN PELT & MAYBURY, ARCHITECTS

GENERAL VIEW

TERRACE

GARDEN FRONT

RESIDENCE FOR MR. JAMES SCRIPPS-BOOTH, LINDA VISTA, CALIFORNIA

MARSTON, VAN PELT & MAYBURY, ARCHITECTS

PERGOLA DETAIL

END GABLE DETAIL

RESIDENCE FOR MR. JAMES SCRIPPS-BOOTH, LINDA VISTA, CALIFORNIA

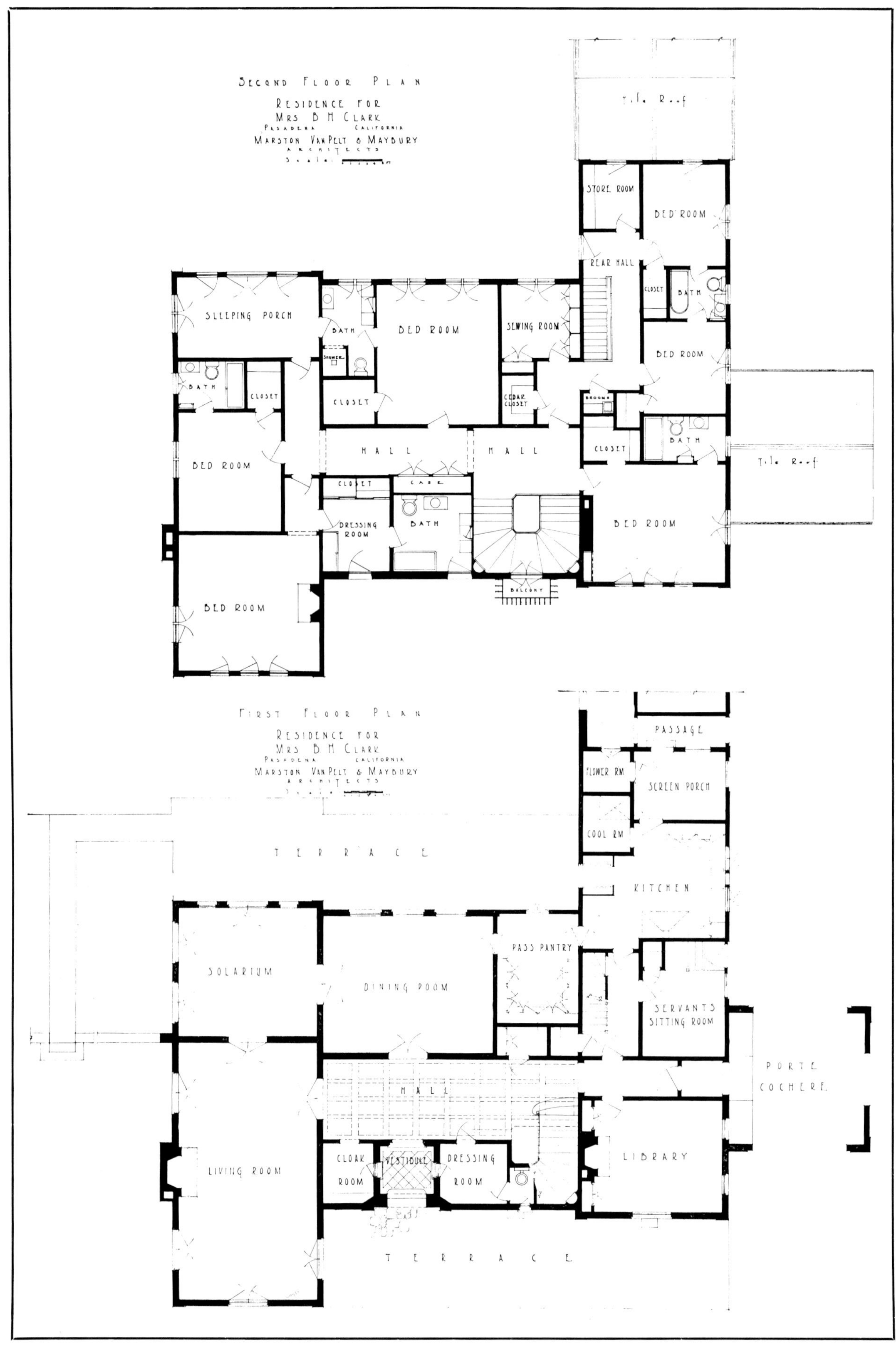

PLANS

RESIDENCE FOR MRS. BERTHA HOLT CLARK, PASADENA, CALIFORNIA

MARSTON, VAN PELT & MAYBURY, ARCHITECTS

FRONT FROM ENTRANCE GATE

"CASA CONTENTA" RESIDENCE FOR MRS. BERTHA HOLT CLARK, PASADENA, CALIFORNIA

MARSTON, VAN PELT & MAYBURY, ARCHITECTS

THE POOL

ENTRANCE DETAIL

"CASA CONTENTA" RESIDENCE FOR MRS. BERTHA HOLT CLARK, PASADENA, CALIFORNIA

MARSTON, VAN PELT & MAYBURY, ARCHITECTS

THE GARDEN "CASA CONTENTA" RESIDENCE FOR MRS. BERTHA HOLT CLARK, PASADENA, CALIFORNIA
MARSTON, VAN PELT & MAYBURY, ARCHITECTS

PLAN

TERRACE

RESIDENCE FOR MRS. EDWARD CUNNINGHAM, MONTECITO, CALIFORNIA

GEORGE WASHINGTON SMITH, ARCHITECT

DRIVE AND ENTRANCE GATE

RESIDENCE FOR MRS. MARY STEWART, MONTECITO, CALIFORNIA

GEORGE WASHINGTON SMITH, ARCHITECT

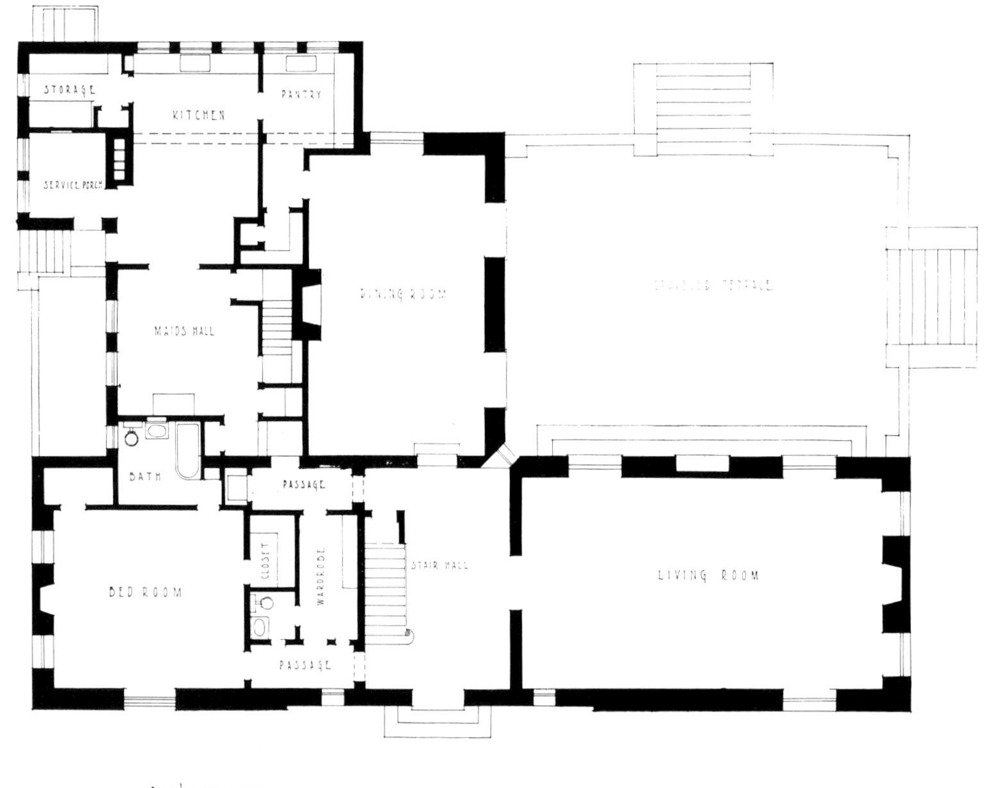

PLAN

ENTRANCE GATE

RESIDENCE FOR MRS. MARY STEWART, MONTECITO, CALIFORNIA

GEORGE WASHINGTON SMITH, ARCHITECT

VIEW

RESIDENCE FOR MRS. MARY STEWART, MONTECITO, CALIFORNIA

GEORGE WASHINGTON SMITH, ARCHITECT

THE GARDEN

RESIDENCE FOR MRS. MARY STEWART, MONTECITO, CALIFORNIA

GEORGE WASHINGTON SMITH, ARCHITECT

DETAIL

DETAIL

RESIDENCE FOR MRS. MARY STEWART, MONTECITO, CALIFORNIA

GEORGE WASHINGTON SMITH, ARCHITECT

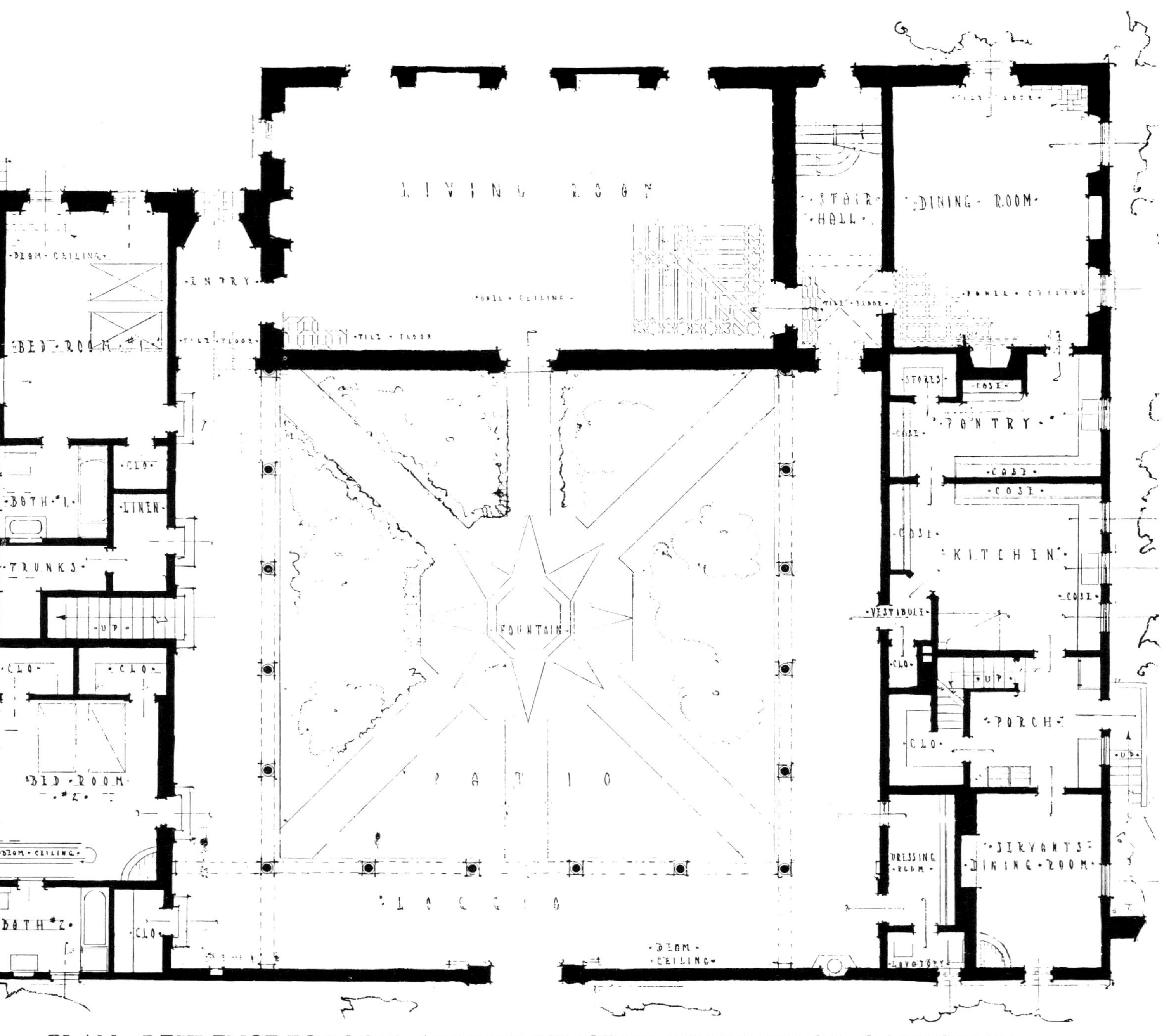

PLAN RESIDENCE FOR MRS. ARTHUR VINCENT, PEBBLE BEACH, CALIFORNIA
GEORGE WASHINGTON SMITH, ARCHITECT

THE TERRACE   RESIDENCE FOR MRS. ARTHUR VINCENT, PEBBLE BEACH, CALIFORNIA
GEORGE WASHINGTON SMITH, ARCHITECT

TERRACE AND BALCONY

TERRACE LOOKING TOWARD THE SEA

RESIDENCE FOR MRS. ARTHUR VINCENT, PEBBLE BEACH, CALIFORNIA

GEORGE WASHINGTON SMITH, ARCHITECT

THE PATIO

RESIDENCE FOR MRS. ARTHUR VINCENT, PEBBLE BEACH, CALIFORNIA

GEORGE WASHINGTON SMITH, ARCHITECT

PATIO, DETAIL

PATIO, DETAIL

RESIDENCE FOR MRS. ARTHUR VINCENT, PEBBLE BEACH, CALIFORNIA

GEORGE WASHINGTON SMITH, ARCHITECT

GENERAL VIEW RESIDENCE FOR MR. CRAIG HEBERTON, MONTECITO, CALIFORNIA
GEORGE WASHINGTON SMITH, ARCHITECT

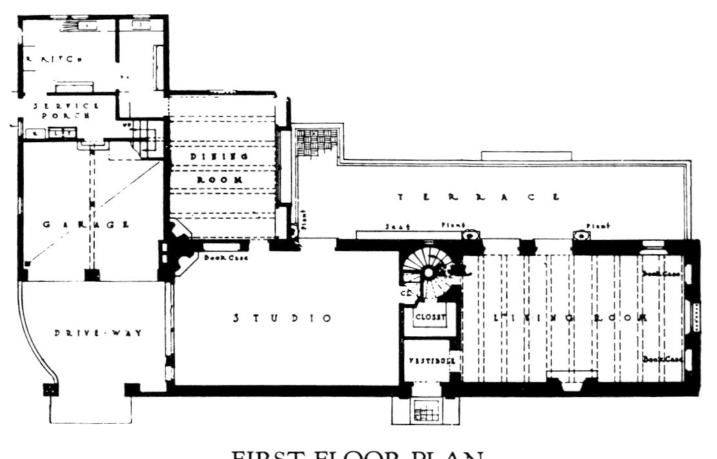

FIRST FLOOR PLAN

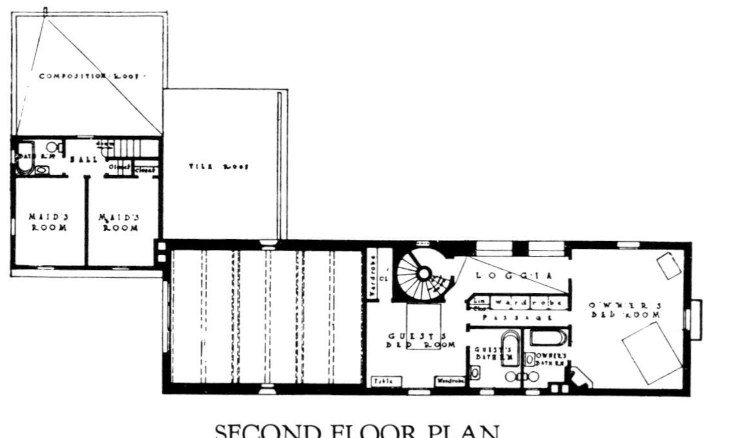

SECOND FLOOR PLAN

DETAIL OF ENTRANCE

RESIDENCE FOR MR. CRAIG HEBERTON, MONTECITO, CALIFORNIA

GEORGE WASHINGTON SMITH, ARCHITECT

GARAGE ENTRANCE

DETAIL SHOWING BALCONY

RESIDENCE FOR MR. CRAIG HEBERTON, MONTECITO, CALIFORNIA

GEORGE WASHINGTON SMITH, ARCHITECT

GARDEN FACADE RESIDENCE FOR MR. CRAIG HEBERTON, MONTECITO, CALIFORNIA

GEORGE WASHINGTON SMITH, ARCHITECT

THE GARDEN

RESIDENCE FOR MR. CRAIG HEBERTON, MONTECITO, CALIFORNIA

GEORGE WASHINGTON SMITH, ARCHITECT

GARDEN DETAIL

GARDEN DETAIL

RESIDENCE FOR MR. CRAIG HEBERTON, MONTECITO, CALIFORNIA

GEORGE WASHINGTON SMITH, ARCHITECT

ENTRANCE PATIO

ENTRANCE GATE

RESIDENCE FOR MR. GEORGE WASHINGTON SMITH, SANTA BARBARA, CALIFORNIA

GEORGE WASHINGTON SMITH, ARCHITECT

IRON WINDOW GRILLE

ENTRANCE GATE

PATIO

RESIDENCE FOR MR. GEORGE WASHINGTON SMITH, SANTA BARBARA, CALIFORNIA

GEORGE WASHINGTON SMITH, ARCHITECT

GARDEN ELEVATION

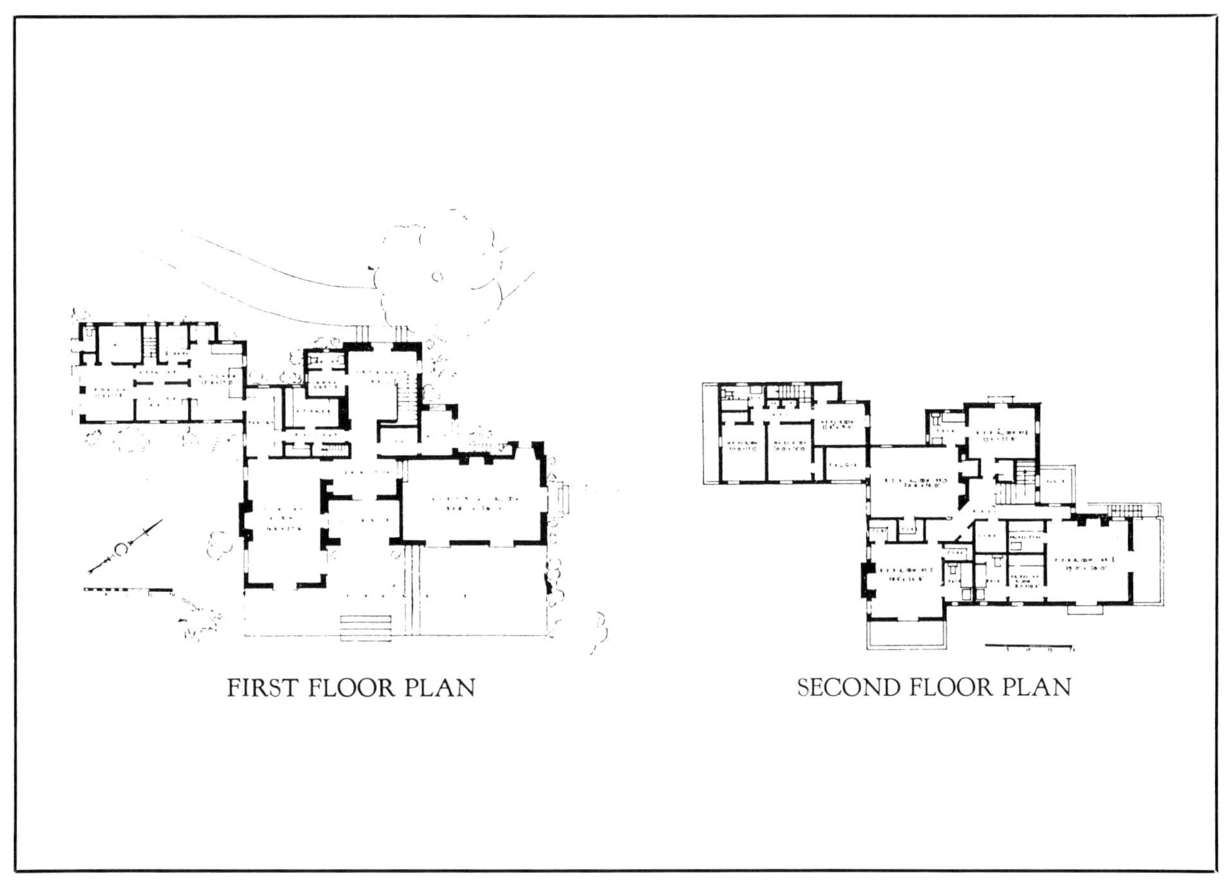

FIRST FLOOR PLAN

SECOND FLOOR PLAN

RESIDENCE FOR MR. DeWITT PARSHALL, SANTA BARBARA, CALIFORNIA

GEORGE WASHINGTON SMITH, ARCHITECT

DETAIL OF PORCH

ENTRANCE FRONT

ENTRANCE FRONT

ENTRANCE DETAIL

RESIDENCE FOR MR. DeWITT PARSHALL, SANTA BARBARA, CALIFORNIA

GEORGE WASHINGTON SMITH, ARCHITECT

EAST ELEVATION

SERVICE WING

RESIDENCE FOR MR. WILLARD P. LINDLEY, SANTA BARBARA, CALIFORNIA

GEORGE WASHINGTON SMITH, ARCHITECT

FRONT ELEVATION RESIDENCE FOR MR. IRVING WRIGHT, SANTA BARBARA, CALIFORNIA
GEORGE WASHINGTON SMITH, ARCHITECT

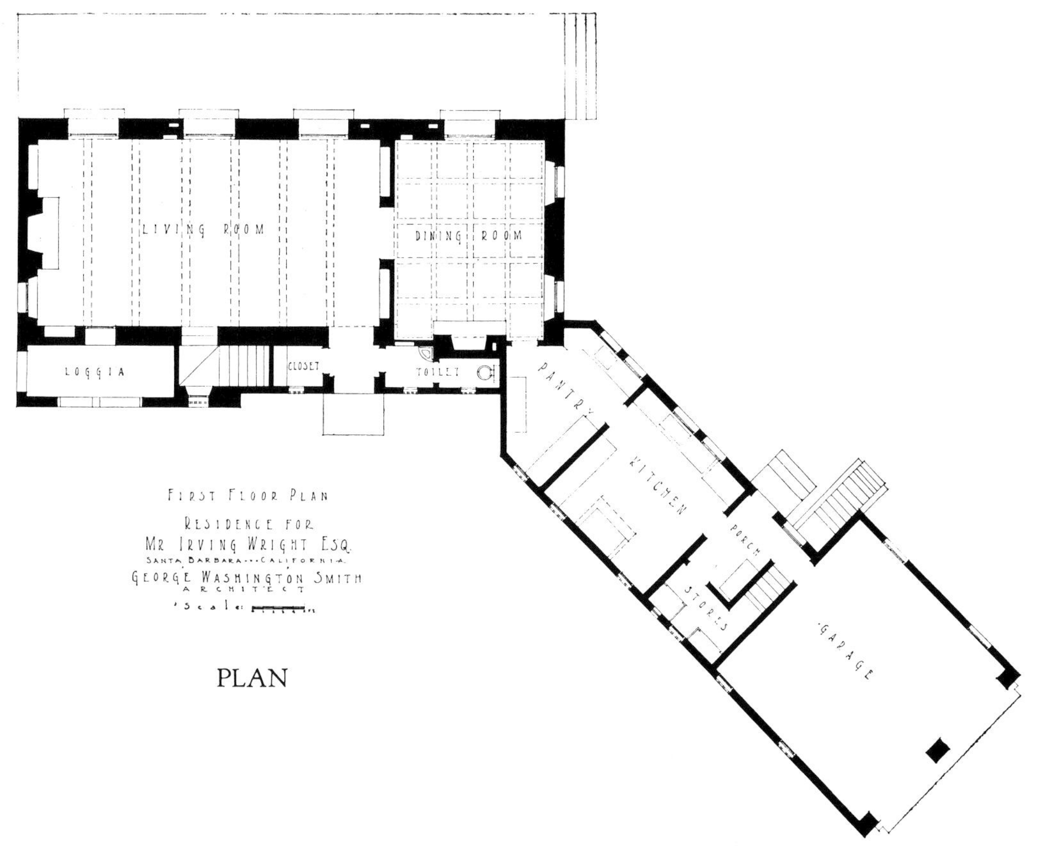

PLAN

TERRACE

RESIDENCE FOR MR. IRVING WRIGHT, SANTA BARBARA, CALIFORNIA

GEORGE WASHINGTON SMITH, ARCHITECT

TERRACE FACADE

RESIDENCE FOR MR. IRVING WRIGHT, SANTA BARBARA, CALIFORNIA

GEORGE WASHINGTON SMITH, ARCHITECT

DINING ROOM RESIDENCE FOR MR. IRVING WRIGHT, SANTA BARBARA, CALIFORNIA
GEORGE WASHINGTON SMITH, ARCHITECT

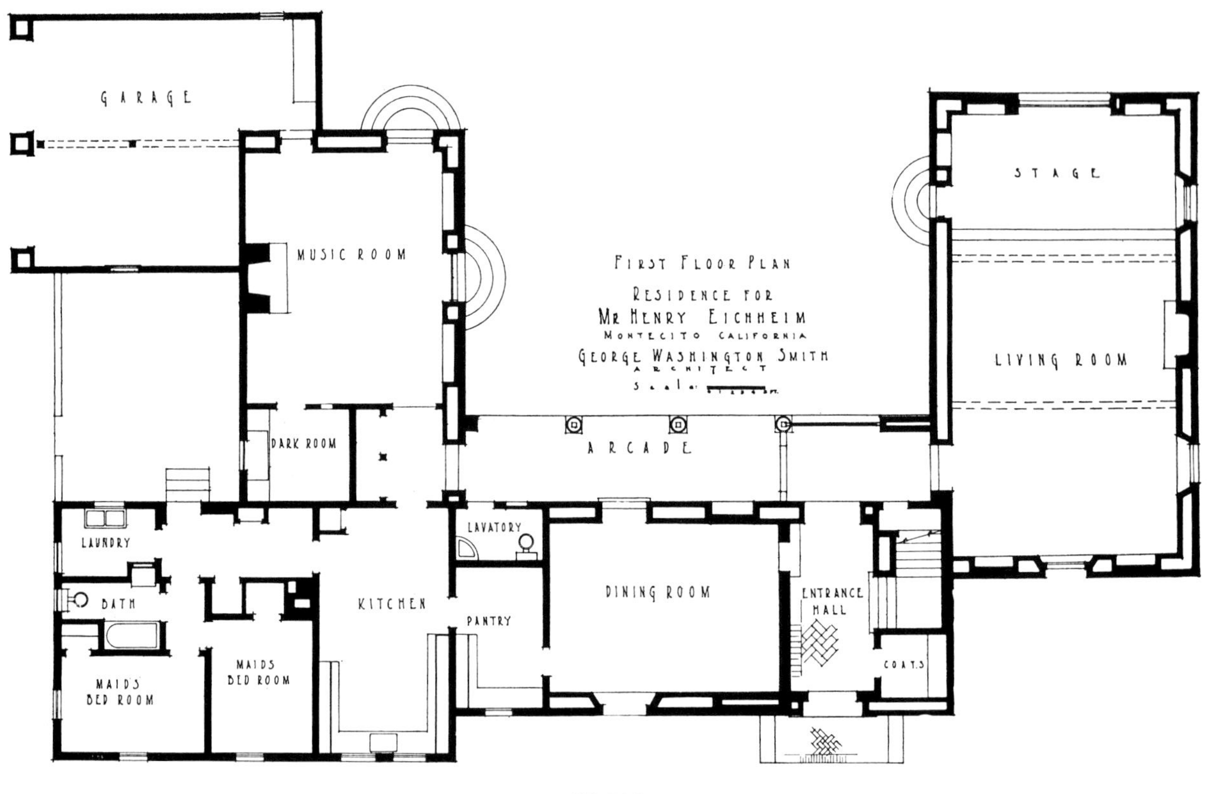

PLAN

PATIO

RESIDENCE FOR MR. HENRY EICHHEIM, MONTECITO, CALIFORNIA

GEORGE WASHINGTON SMITH, ARCHITECT

GENERAL VIEW "DIAS DORADOS", RESIDENCE FOR MR. THOMAS H. INCE, BEVERLY HILLS, CALIFORNIA

ROY SHELDON PRICE, ARCHITECT

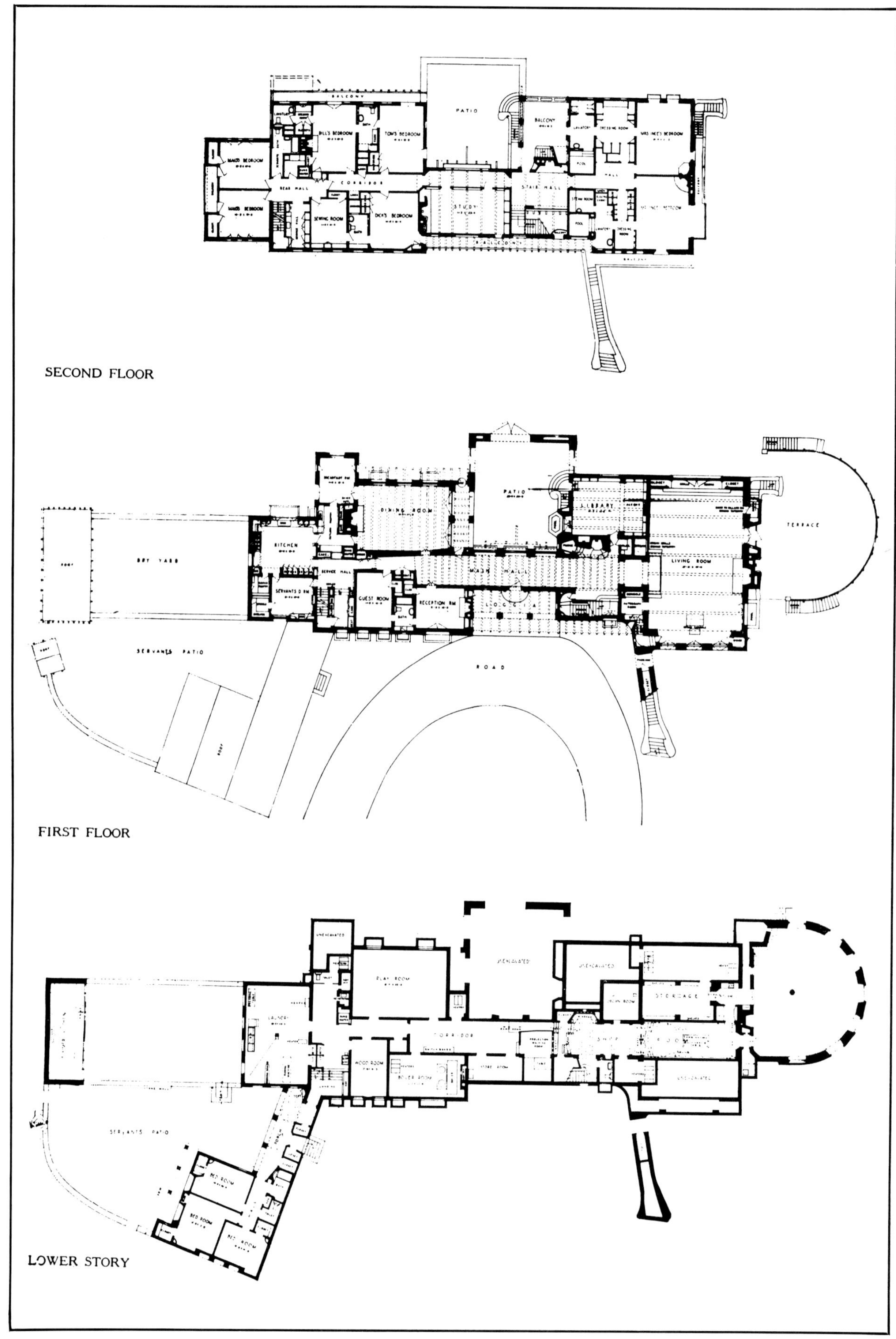

FLOOR PLANS "DIAS DORADOS"

RESIDENCE FOR MR. THOMAS H. INCE, BEVERLY HILLS, CALIFORNIA

ROY SHELDON PRICE, ARCHITECT

VIEW ACROSS THE POOL

"DIAS DORADOS", RESIDENCE FOR MR. THOMAS H. INCE, BEVERLY HILLS, CALIFORNIA

ROY SHELDON PRICE, ARCHITECT

PERGOLA

OLD WELL, DRYING YARD AND SERVICE ENTRANCE, "DIAS DORADOS"

RESIDENCE FOR MR. THOMAS H. INCE, BEVERLY HILLS, CALIFORNIA

ROY SHELDON PRICE, ARCHITECT

DOVE COTE

DETAIL OF BALCONY

"DIAS DORADOS", RESIDENCE FOR MR. THOMAS H. INCE, BEVERLY HILLS, CALIFORNIA

ROY SHELDON PRICE, ARCHITECT

VIEW IN GROUNDS SHOWING DOVE COTE

"DIAS DORADOS", RESIDENCE FOR MR. THOMAS H. INCE, BEVERLY HILLS, CALIFORNIA

ROY SHELDON PRICE, ARCHITECT

ENTRANCE GATE

GARAGE, "DIAS DORADOS"

RESIDENCE FOR MR. THOMAS H. INCE, BEVERLY HILLS, CALIFORNIA

ROY SHELDON PRICE, ARCHITECT

THE SMITHY

DUCK HOUSE AND POOL, "DIAS DORADOS"

RESIDENCE FOR MR. THOMAS H. INCE, BEVERLY HILLS, CALIFORNIA

ROY SHELDON PRICE, ARCHITECT

MOTION PICTURE PROJECTION ROOM

LIBRARY, "DIAS DORADOS"

RESIDENCE FOR MR. THOMAS H. INCE, BEVERLY HILLS, CALIFORNIA

ROY SHELDON PRICE, ARCHITECT

GENERAL VIEW RESIDENCE FOR MR. GEORGE C. REW, CORONADO, CALIFORNIA
ELMER GREY, ARCHITECT

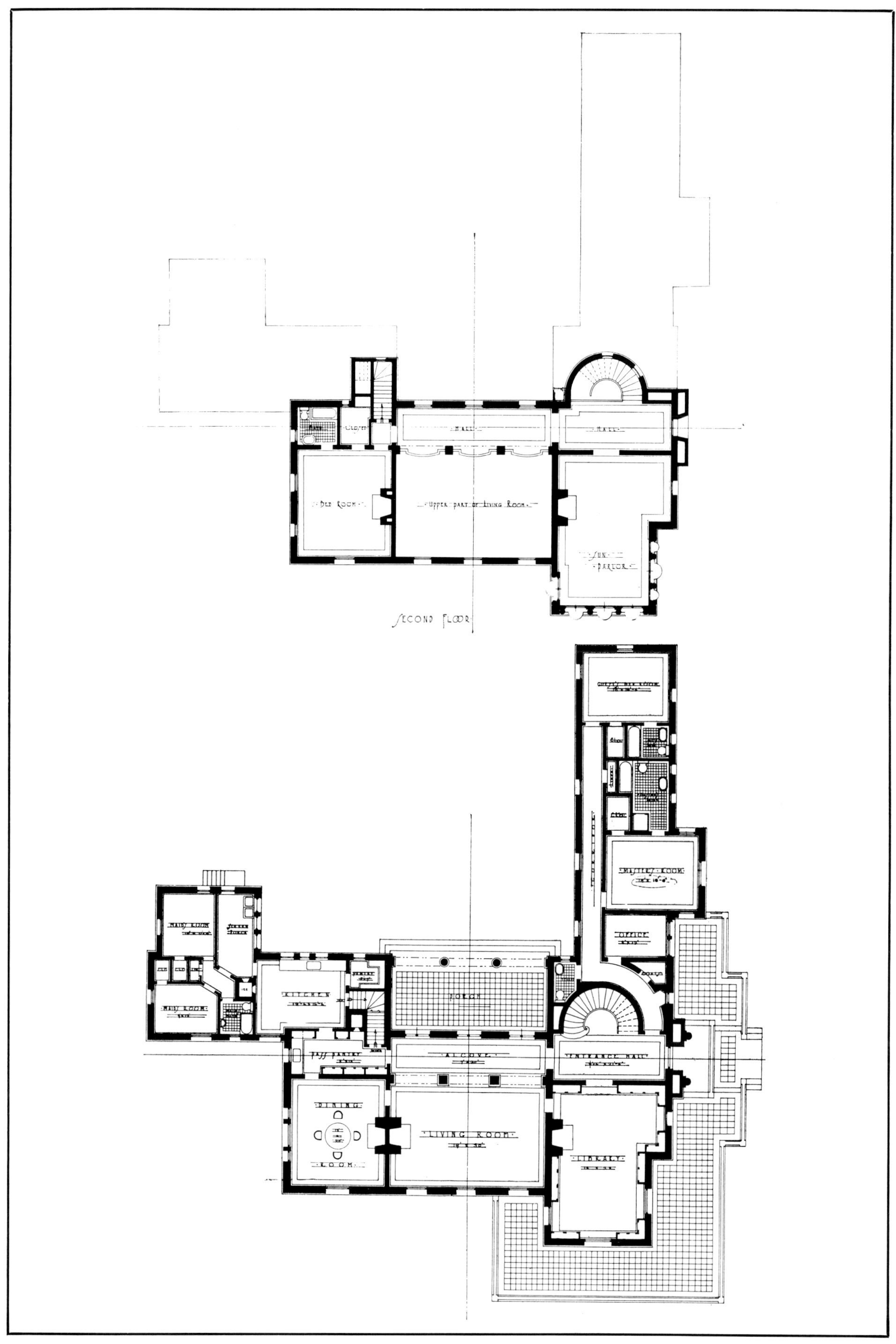

PLANS

RESIDENCE FOR MR. GEORGE C. REW, CORONADO, CALIFORNIA

ELMER GREY, ARCHITECT

ENTRANCE DETAIL

PLANS RESIDENCE FOR MR. GEORGE C. REW, CORONADO, CALIFORNIA

ELMER GREY, ARCHITECT

GENERAL VIEW FROM STREET

FACADE DETAIL

DOOR DETAIL

RESIDENCE FOR MR. MERRITT H. ADAMSON, LOS ANGELES, CALIFORNIA

ELMER GREY, ARCHITECT

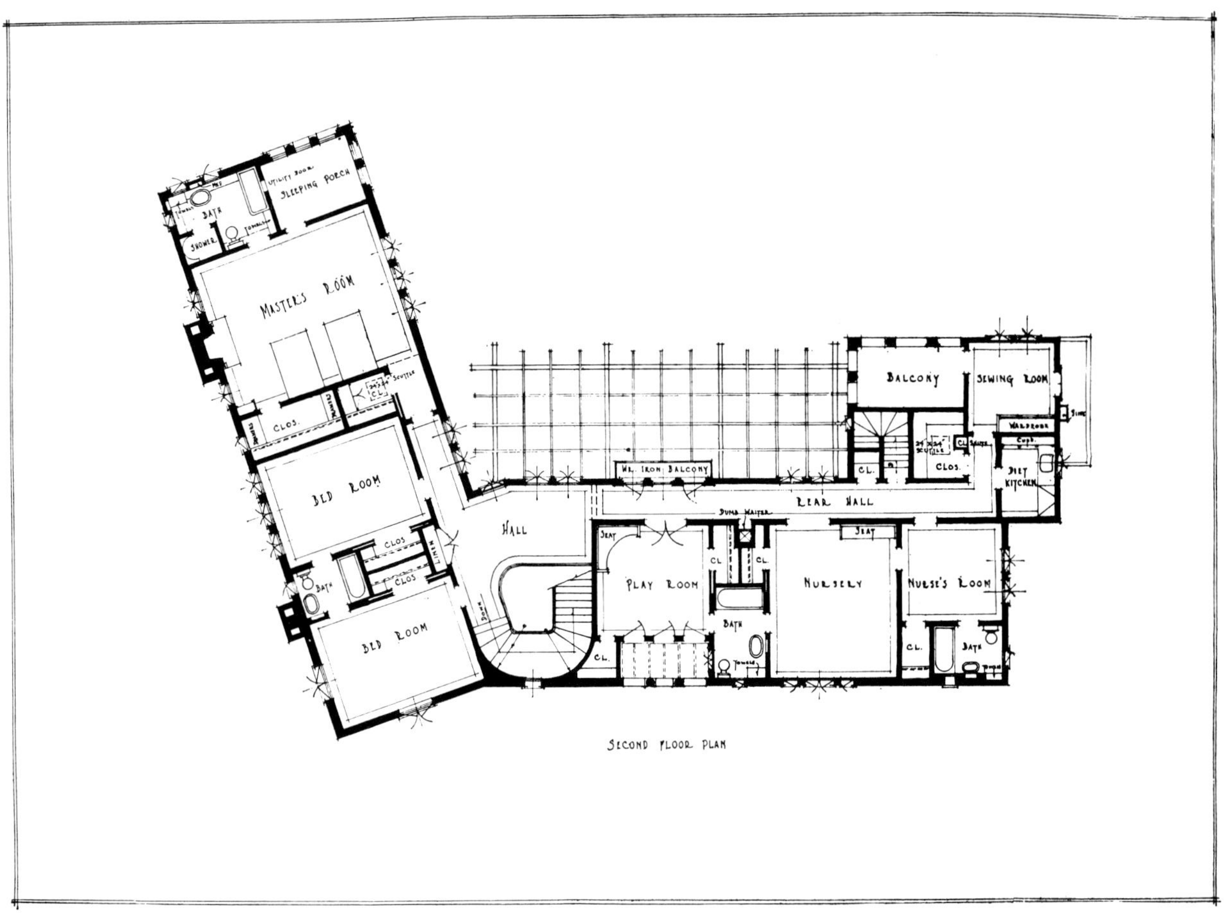

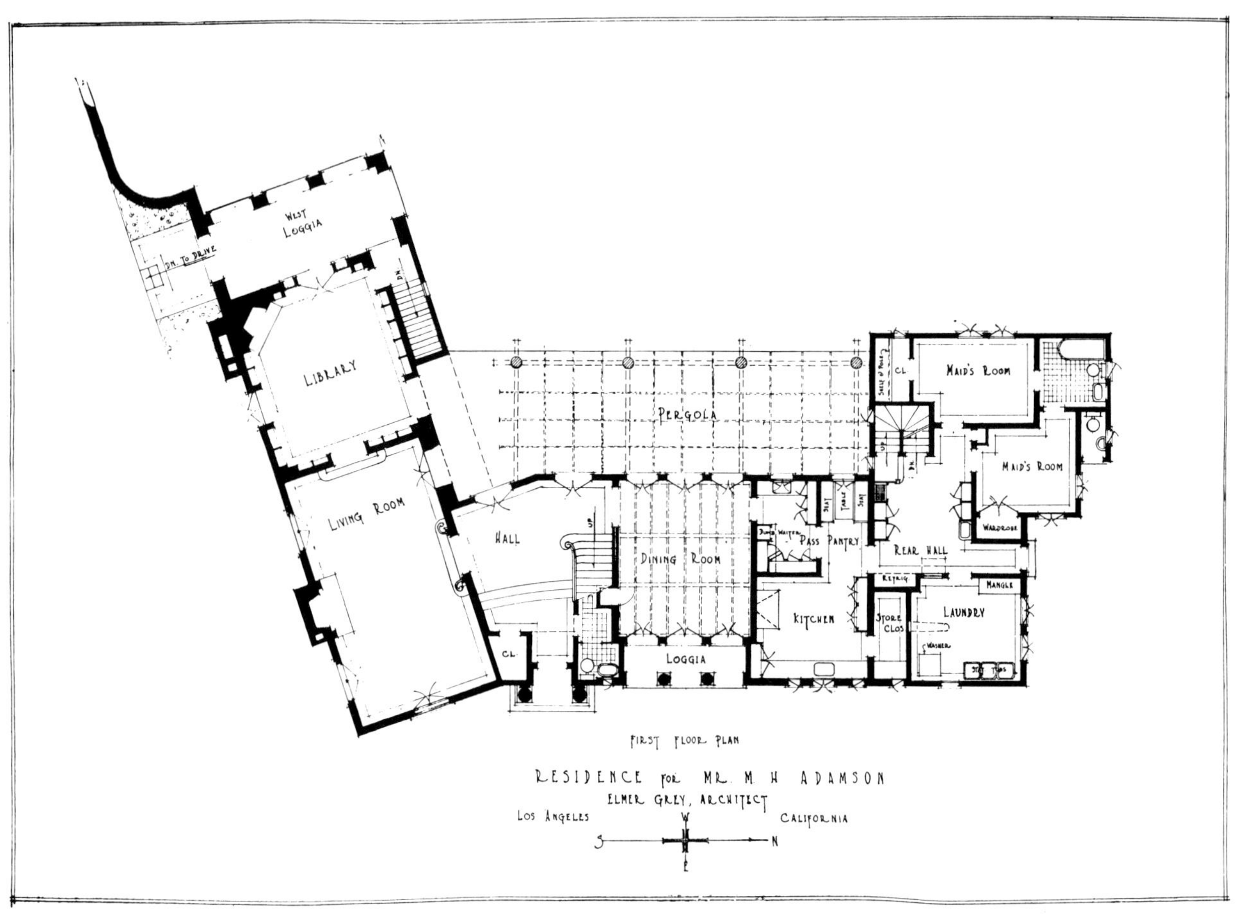

PLANS

RESIDENCE FOR MR. MERRITT H. ADAMSON, LOS ANGELES, CALIFORNIA

ELMER GREY, ARCHITECT

DETAIL

DETAIL

RESIDENCE FOR MR. MERRITT H. ADAMSON, LOS ANGELES, CALIFORNIA

ELMER GREY, ARCHITECT

FRONT FACADE

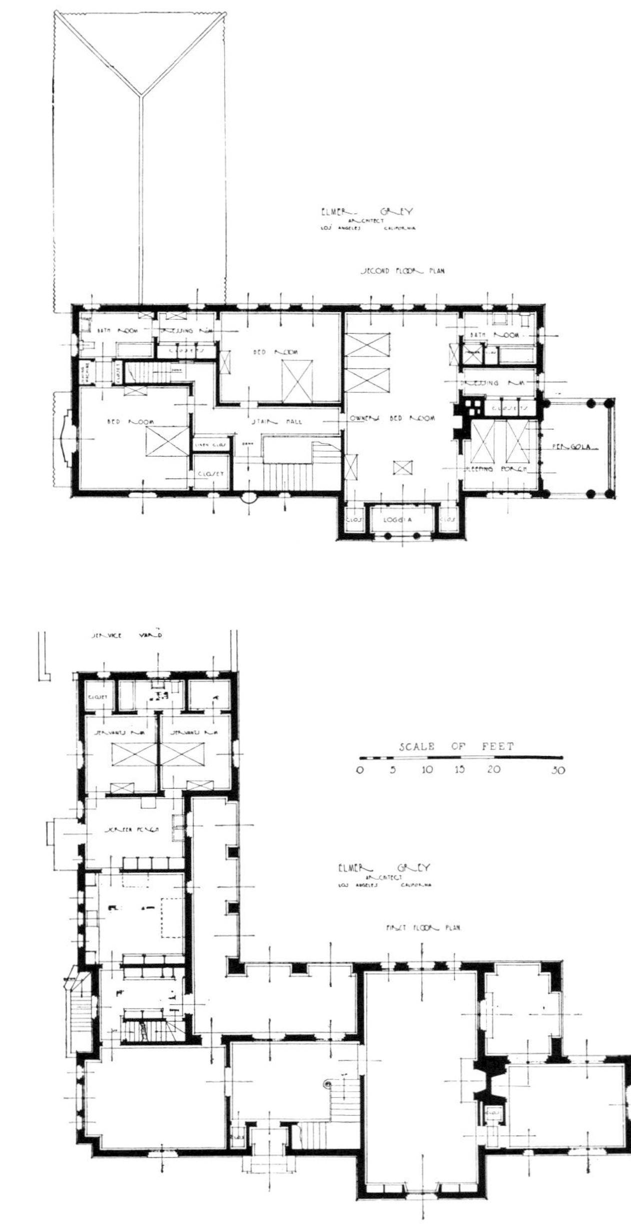

PLANS

RESIDENCE FOR ROGER GOODIN, LOS ANGELES, CALIFORNIA

ELMER GREY, ARCHITECT

FACADE

PATIO

ENTRANCE PORCH

RESIDENCE FOR MR. HENRY W. SCHULTZ, PASADENA, CALIFORNIA

ELMER GREY, ARCHITECT

GENERAL VIEW

OCEAN FRONT

RESIDENCE FOR MRS. CHARLES W. CLARK, SAN MATEO, CALIFORNIA

BAKEWELL & BROWN, ARCHITECTS

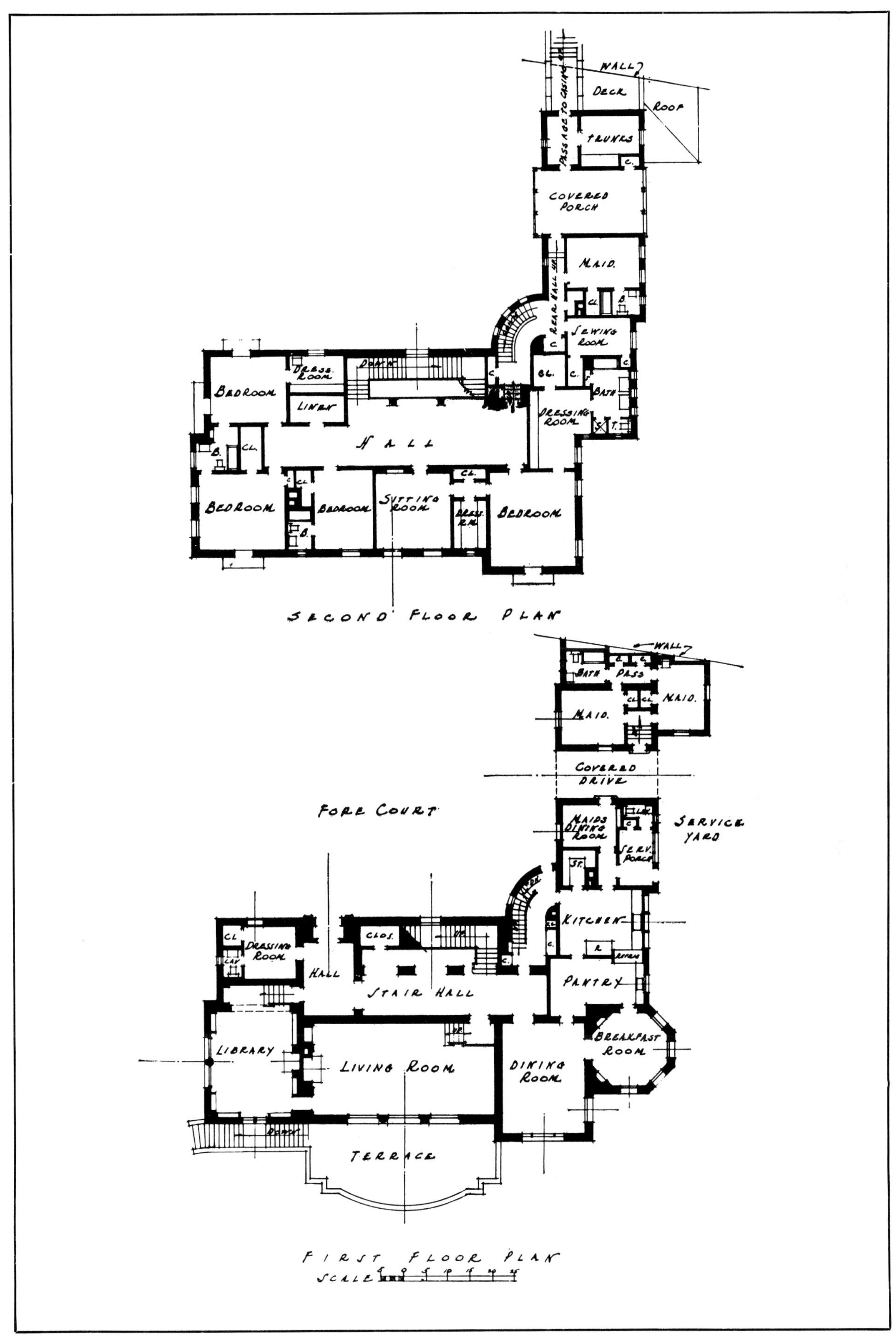

PLANS

RESIDENCE FOR MR. BEN R. MEYER, BEVERLY HILLS, CALIFORNIA

JOHNSON, KAUFMAN & COATE, ARCHITECTS

FACADE

RESIDENCE FOR MR. BEN R. MEYER, BEVERLY HILLS, CALIFORNIA

JOHNSON, KAUFMANN & COATE, ARCHITECTS

ENTRANCE AND FACADE DETAIL

FORECOURT AND FOUNTAIN

RESIDENCE FOR MR. BEN R. MEYER, BEVERLY HILLS, CALIFORNIA

JOHNSON, KAUFMANN & COATE, ARCHITECTS

FACADE AND TERRACE RESIDENCE FOR MR. J. O. STOKES, BRENTWOOD, CALIFORNIA
JOHN AND DONALD B. PARKINSON, ARCHITECTS

PATIO RESIDENCE FOR MR. J. O. STOKES, BRENTWOOD, CALIFORNIA
JOHN AND DONALD B. PARKINSON, ARCHITECTS

LIVING ROOM DOORWAY

GARDEN ENTRANCE TO PATIO

RESIDENCE FOR MR. DONALD B. PARKINSON, SANTA MONICA, CALIFORNIA

JOHN AND DONALD B. PARKINSON, ARCHITECTS

GENERAL VIEW

GENERAL VIEW

RESIDENCE FOR MR. DONALD B. PARKINSON, SANTA MONICA, CALIFORNIA

JOHN AND DONALD B. PARKINSON, ARCHITECTS

FRONT

DETAIL OF FRONT

RESIDENCE FOR MR. ARTHUR K. BOURNE, PASADENA, CALIFORNIA

WALLACE NEFF, ARCHITECT

DETAIL OF REAR WING

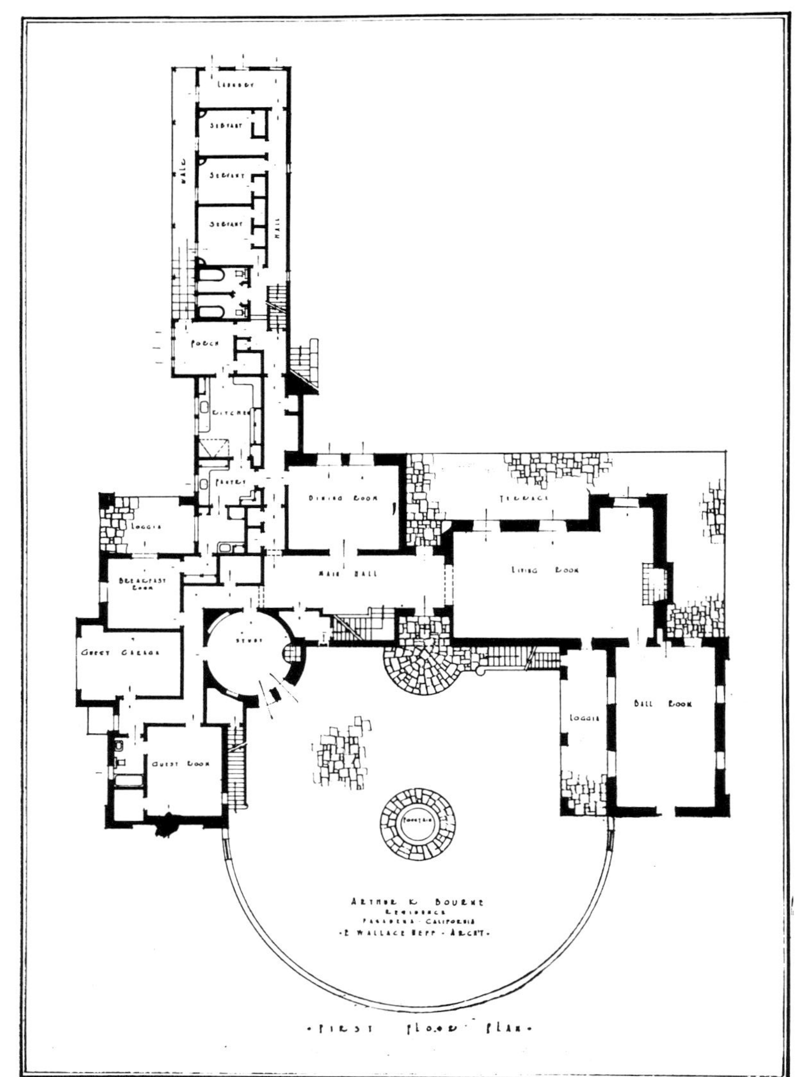

FIRST FLOOR PLAN

RESIDENCE FOR MR. ARTHUR K. BOURNE, PASADENA, CALIFORNIA

WALLACE NEFF, ARCHITECT

DETAIL OF TERRACE PORCH

DETAIL OF TERRACE AND STAIRCASE

RESIDENCE FOR MR. ARTHUR K. BOURNE, PASADENA, CALIFORNIA

WALLACE NEFF, ARCHITECT

DETAIL OF TERRACE AND DOORWAY

DETAIL OF STAIRWAY AND BALCONY

RESIDENCE FOR MR. ARTHUR K. BOURNE, PASADENA, CALIFORNIA

WALLACE NEFF, ARCHITECT

ENTRANCE HALL

DETAIL OF TILE STAIRCASE

RESIDENCE FOR MR. ARTHUR K. BOURNE, PASADENA, CALIFORNIA

WALLACE NEFF, ARCHITECT

GENERAL VIEW

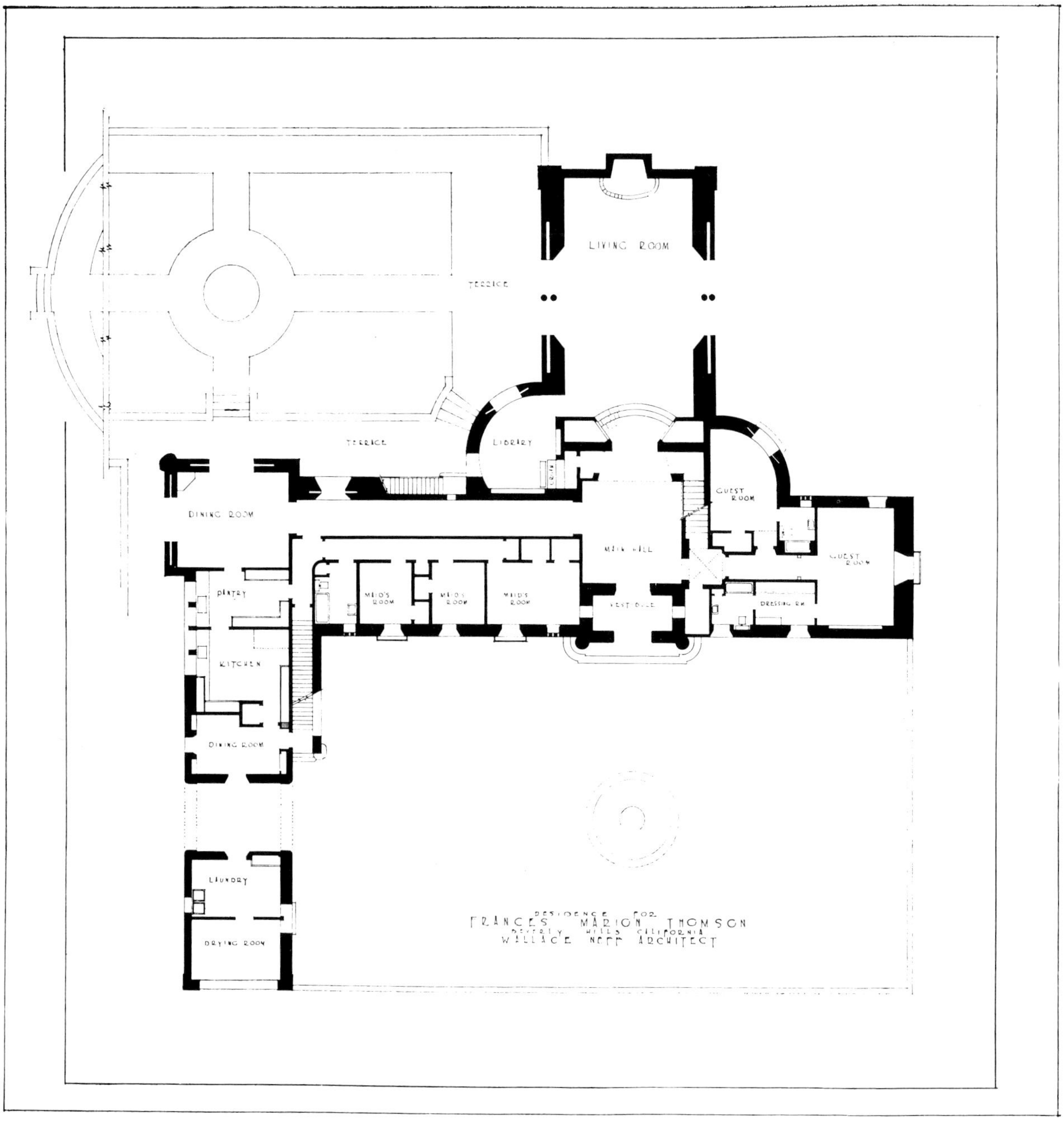

PLAN

RESIDENCE FOR MRS. FRANCES MARION THOMSON, BEVERLY HILLS, CALIFORNIA

WALLACE NEFF, ARCHITECT

ENTRANCE COURT, SERVICE WING

LIVING ROOM WING

RESIDENCE FOR MRS. FRANCES MARION THOMSON, BEVERLY HILLS, CALIFORNIA

WALLACE NEFF, ARCHITECT

PATIO, TERRACE

SERVICE WING, STAIRCASE

RESIDENCE FOR MRS. FRANCES MARION THOMSON, BEVERLY HILLS, CALIFORNIA

WALLACE NEFF, ARCHITECT

PATIO, FOUNTAIN

RESIDENCE FOR MRS. FRANCES MARION THOMSON, BEVERLY HILLS, CALIFORNIA

WALLACE NEFF, ARCHITECT

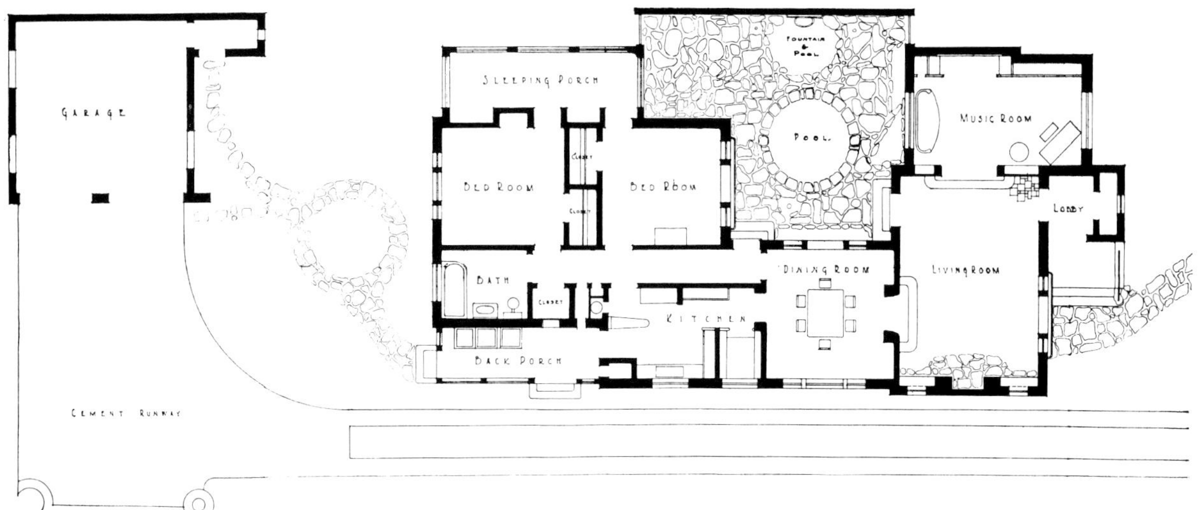

PLAN

FRONT ENTRANCE

RESIDENCE FOR MR. R. B. KEELER, SOUTH GATE, CALIFORNIA

R. B. KEELER, ARCHITECT

PATIO

PATIO, GATE

PATIO, WALL FOUNTAIN

RESIDENCE FOR MR. R. B. KEELER, SOUTH GATE, CALIFORNIA

R. B. KEELER, ARCHITECT

CORNER OF PATIO

RESIDENCE FOR MR. R. B. KEELER, SOUTH GATE, CALIFORNIA

R. B. KEELER, ARCHITECT

WINDOW DETAIL

WINDOW DETAIL

RESIDENCE FOR MR. R. B. KEELER, SOUTH GATE, CALIFORNIA

R. B. KEELER, ARCHITECT

REAR PORCH AND GARAGE

SLEEPING PORCH, BEDS FOLDED UP INTO WALL

RESIDENCE FOR MR. R. B. KEELER, SOUTH GATE, CALIFORNIA

R. B. KEELER, ARCHITECT

DINING ROOM RESIDENCE FOR MR. R. B. KEELER, SOUTH GATE, CALIFORNIA

R. B. KEELER, ARCHITECT

DINING ROOM DETAIL

ENTRY

BREAKFAST NOOK

RESIDENCE FOR MR. R. B. KEELER, SOUTH GATE, CALIFORNIA

R. B. KEELER, ARCHITECT

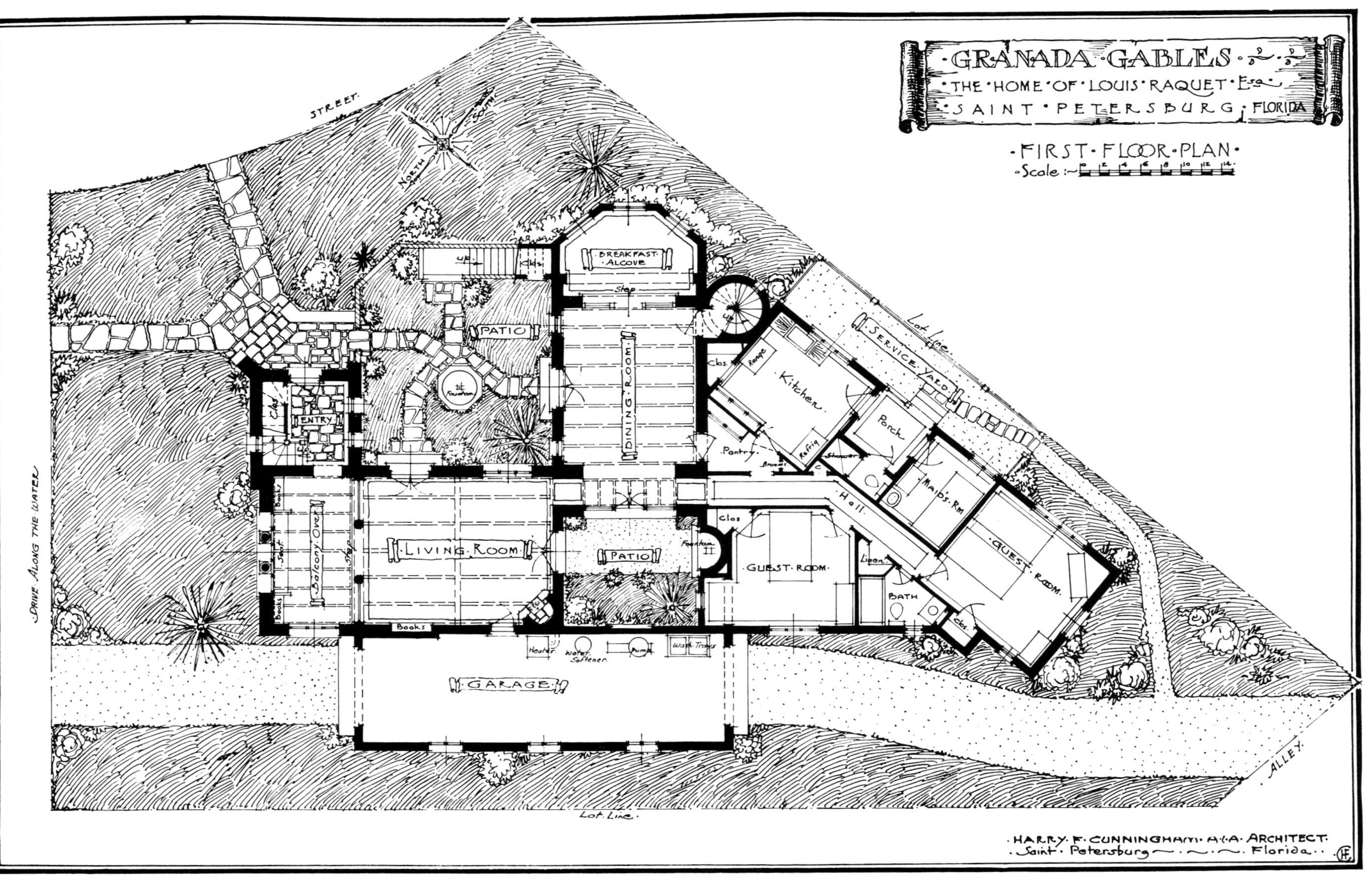

PLAN OF FIRST FLOOR AND GROUNDS

"GRANADA GABLES", RESIDENCE FOR MR. LOUIS RAQUET, ST. PETERSBURG, FLORIDA

HARRY F. CUNNINGHAM, ARCHITECT

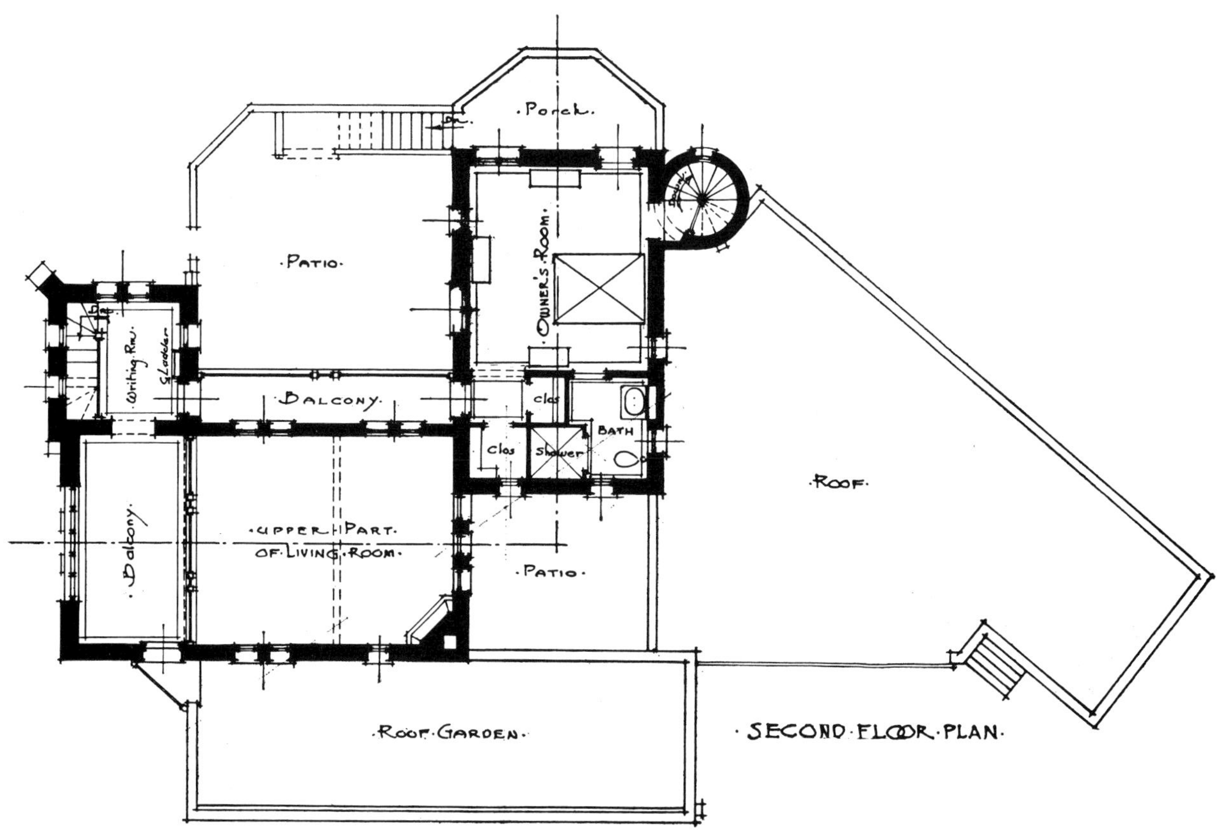

SECOND FLOOR PLAN, "GRANADA GABLES"

NORTHWEST FRONT

"GRANADA GABLES"
RESIDENCE FOR MR. LOUIS RAQUET, ST. PETERSBURG, FLORIDA
HARRY F. CUNNINGHAM, ARCHITECT

SOUTHEAST FRONT

"GRANADA GABLES", RESIDENCE FOR MR. LOUIS RAQUET, ST. PETERSBURG, FLORIDA

HARRY F. CUNNINGHAM, ARCHITECT

LARGE PATIO, FOUNTAIN

ARCHES LOOKING INTO LIVING ROOM

"GRANADA GABLES", RESIDENCE FOR MR. LOUIS RAQUET, ST. PETERSBURG, FLORIDA
HARRY F. CUNNINGHAM, ARCHITECT

ENTRANCE GATE, "CASA ALEXANDRO"

RESIDENCE FOR MR. GEORGE ALEXANDER McKINLOCK, PALM BEACH, FLORIDA

MARION SIMS WYETH, ARCHITECT

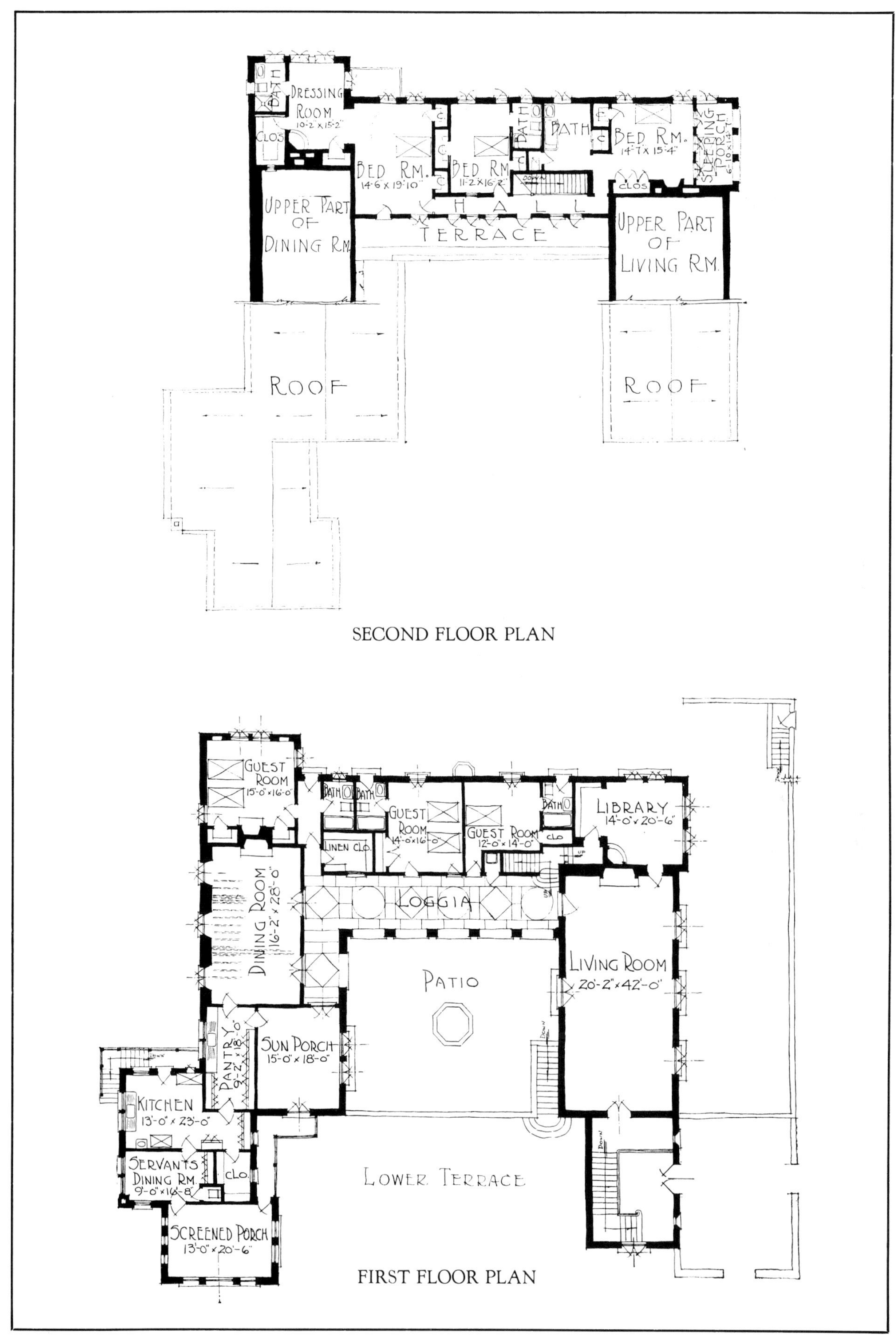

SECOND FLOOR PLAN

FIRST FLOOR PLAN

"CASA ALEXANDRO"

RESIDENCE FOR MR. GEORGE ALEXANDER McKINLOCK, PALM BEACH, FLORIDA

MARION SIMS WYETH, ARCHITECT

ENTRANCE COURT AND GATE, "CASA ALEXANDRO"

RESIDENCE FOR MR. GEORGE ALEXANDER McKINLOCK, PALM BEACH, FLORIDA

MARION SIMS WYETH, ARCHITECT

PATIO GATE "CASA ALEXANDRO"

RESIDENCE FOR MR. GEORGE ALEXANDER McKINLOCK, PALM BEACH, FLORIDA

MARION SIMS WYETH, ARCHITECT

PATIO "CASA ALEXANDRO", RESIDENCE FOR MR. GEORGE ALEXANDER McKINLOCK, PALM BEACH, FLORIDA
MARION SIMS WYETH, ARCHITECT

DETAIL OF LOGGIA, "CASA ALEXANDRO"

RESIDENCE FOR MR. GEORGE ALEXANDER McKINLOCK, PALM BEACH, FLORIDA

MARION SIMS WYETH, ARCHITECT

LOWER TERRACE, "CASA ALEXANDRO"

RESIDENCE FOR MR. GEORGE ALEXANDER McKINLOCK, PALM BEACH, FLORIDA

MARION SIMS WYETH, ARCHITECT

LOGGIA INTERIOR, "CASA ALEXANDRO"

RESIDENCE FOR MR. GEORGE ALEXANDER McKINLOCK, PALM BEACH, FLORIDA

MARION SIMS WYETH, ARCHITECT

SALA (LIVING ROOM) "CASA ALEXANDRO"

RESIDENCE FOR MR. GEORGE ALEXANDER McKINLOCK, PALM BEACH, FLORIDA

MARION SIMS WYETH, ARCHITECT

COMEDOR (DINING ROOM) "CASA ALEXANDRO"

RESIDENCE FOR MR. GEORGE ALEXANDER McKINLOCK, PALM BEACH, FLORIDA

MARION SIMS WYETH, ARCHITECT

GENERAL VIEW RESIDENCE FOR MR. FREDERICK S. WHEELER, PALM BEACH, FLORIDA
MARION SIMS WYETH, ARCHITECT

DOORWAY

RESIDENCE FOR MR. FREDERICK S. WHEELER, PALM BEACH, FLORIDA

MARION SIMS WYETH, ARCHITECT

PATIO RESIDENCE FOR MR. FREDERICK S. WHEELER, PALM BEACH, FLORIDA

MARION SIMS WYETH, ARCHITECT

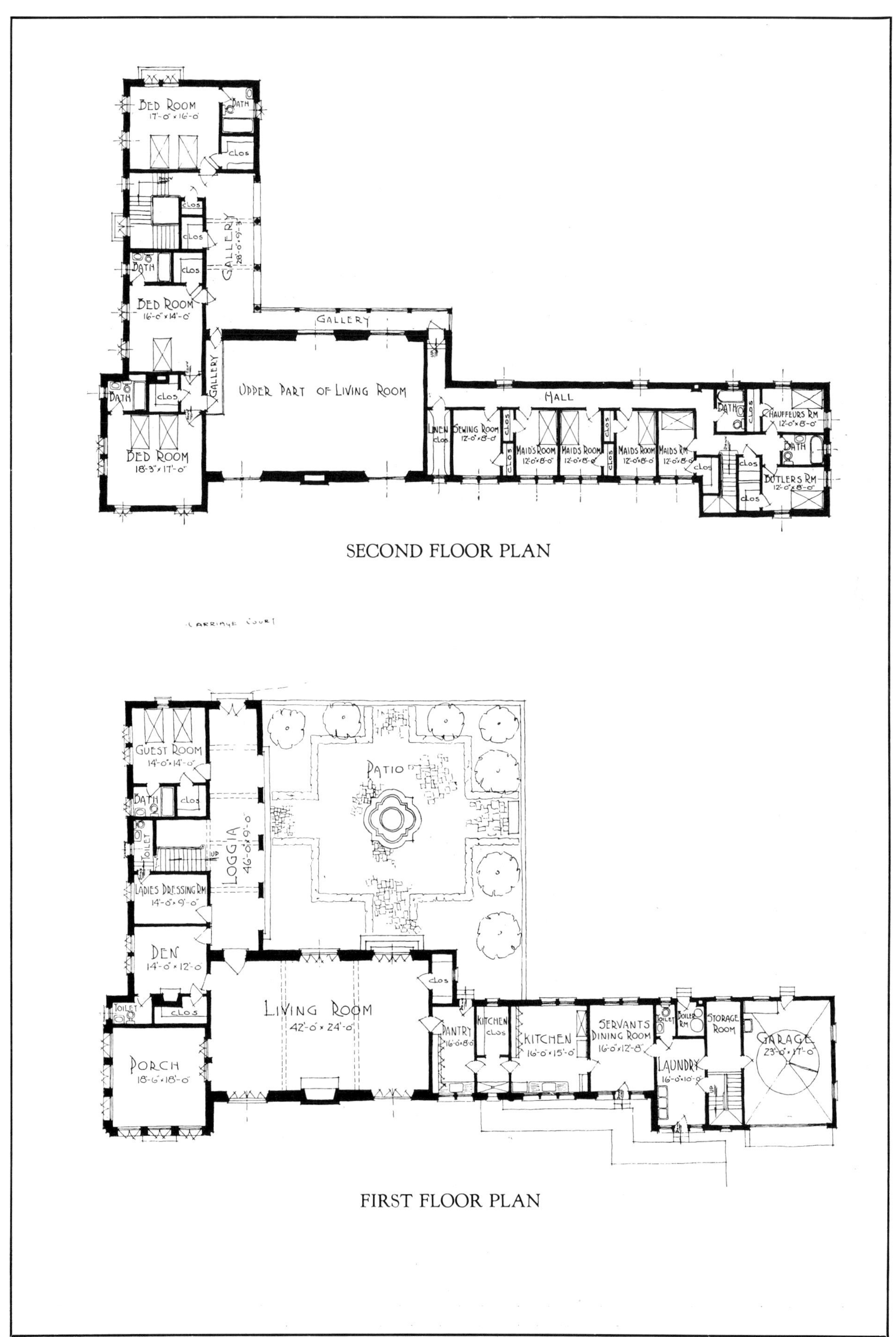

SECOND FLOOR PLAN

FIRST FLOOR PLAN

RESIDENCE FOR MR. FREDERICK S. WHEELER, PALM BEACH, FLORIDA

MARION SIMS WYETH, ARCHITECT

LOGGIA

RESIDENCE FOR MR. FREDERICK S. WHEELER, PALM BEACH, FLORIDA

MARION SIMS WYETH, ARCHITECT

SALA (LIVING-DINING ROOM)

RESIDENCE FOR MR. FREDERICK S. WHEELER, PALM BEACH, FLORIDA

MARION SIMS WYETH, ARCHITECT

SALA (LIVING-DINING ROOM)

RESIDENCE FOR MR. FREDERICK S. WHEELER, PALM BEACH, FLORIDA

MARION SIMS WYETH, ARCHITECT

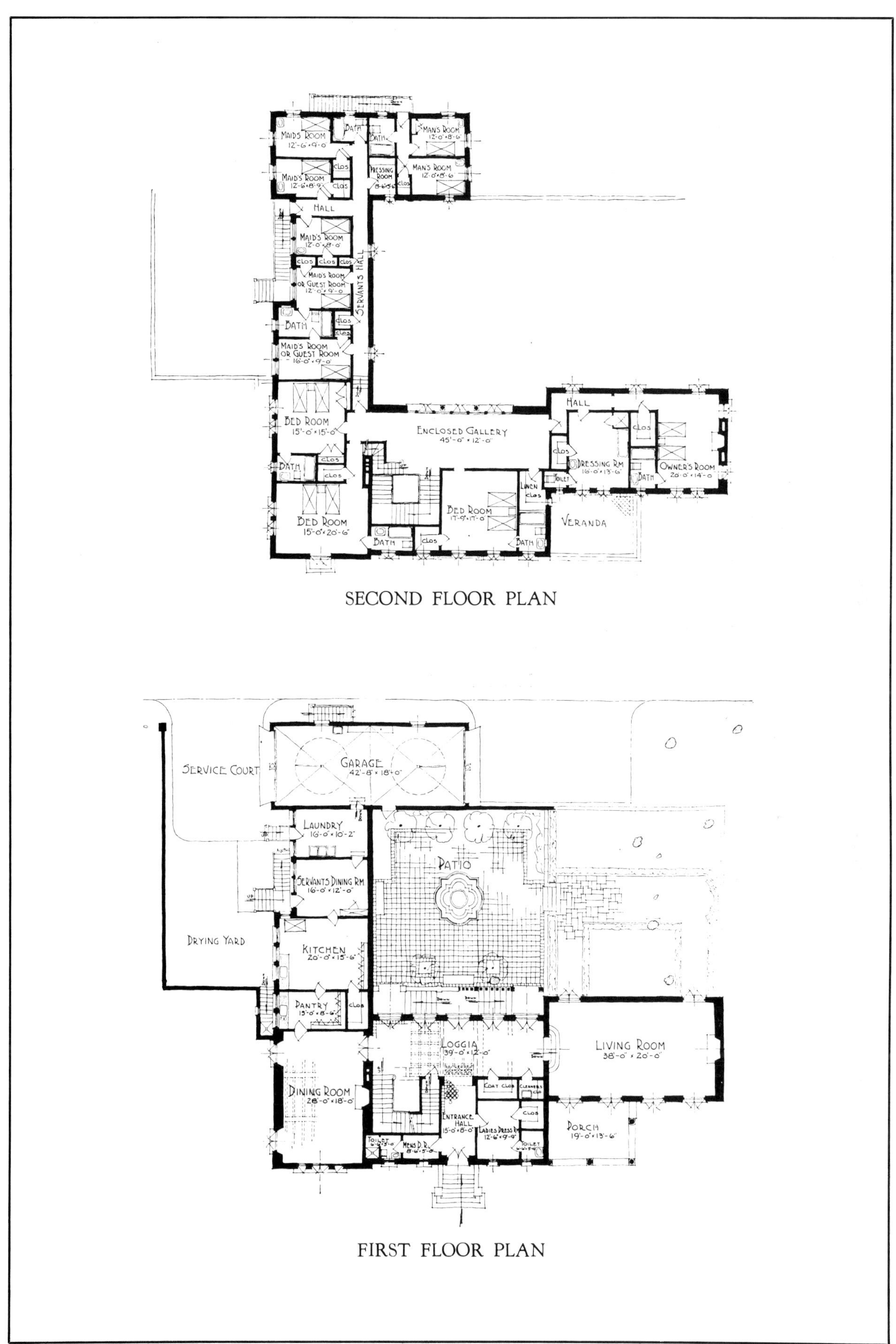

SECOND FLOOR PLAN

FIRST FLOOR PLAN

RESIDENCE FOR MR. CLARENCE H. GEIST, PALM BEACH, FLORIDA

MARION SIMS WYETH, ARCHITECT

FRONT FACADE

PATIO

RESIDENCE FOR MR. CLARENCE H. GEIST, PALM BEACH, FLORIDA

MARION SIMS WYETH, ARCHITECT

PATIO

RESIDENCE FOR MR. CLARENCE H. GEIST, PALM BEACH, FLORIDA

MARION SIMS WYETH, ARCHITECT

LOGGIA

RESIDENCE FOR MR. CLARENCE H. GEIST, PALM BEACH, FLORIDA

MARION SIMS WYETH, ARCHITECT

COMEDOR (DINING ROOM) RESIDENCE FOR MR. CLARENCE H. GEIST, PALM BEACH, FLORIDA

MARION SIMS WYETH, ARCHITECT

PATIO DETAIL

PATIO ENTRANCE

"TRE FONTANE", RESIDENCE FOR MR. MARION SIMS WYETH, PALM BEACH, FLORIDA

MARION SIMS WYETH, ARCHITECT

PATIO "TRE FONTANE"

RESIDENCE FOR MR. MARION SIMS WYETH, PALM BEACH, FLORIDA

MARION SIMS WYETH, ARCHITECT

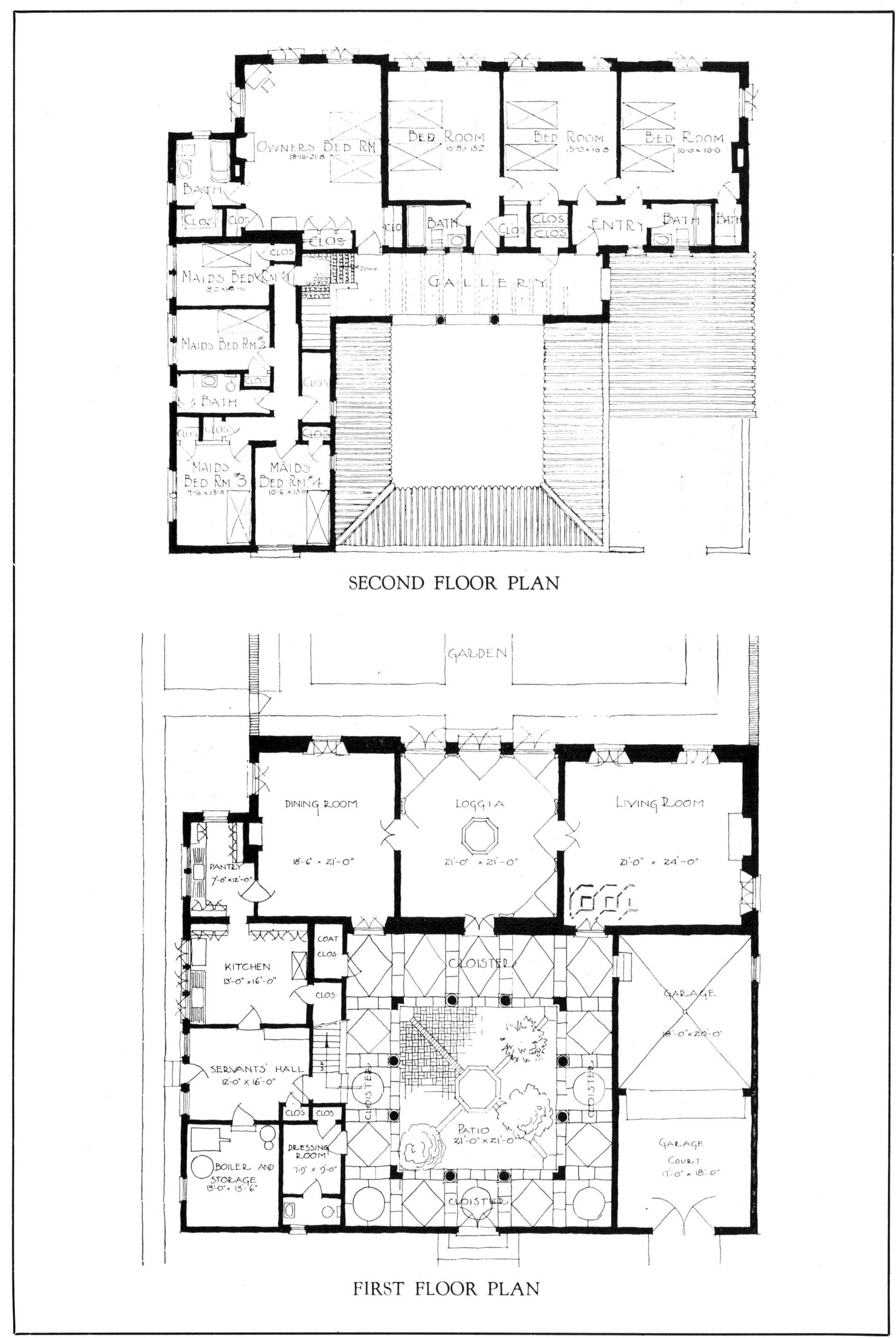

SECOND FLOOR PLAN

FIRST FLOOR PLAN

"TRE FONTANE"

RESIDENCE FOR MR. MARION SIMS WYETH, PALM BEACH, FLORIDA

MARION SIMS WYETH, ARCHITECT

SALA (LIVING ROOM)

"TRE FONTANE", RESIDENCE FOR MR. MARION SIMS WYETH, PALM BEACH, FLORIDA

MARION SIMS WYETH, ARCHITECT

FACADE RESIDENCE FOR MRS. FRANK P. FRAZIER, PALM BEACH, FLORIDA

MARION SIMS WYETH, ARCHITECT

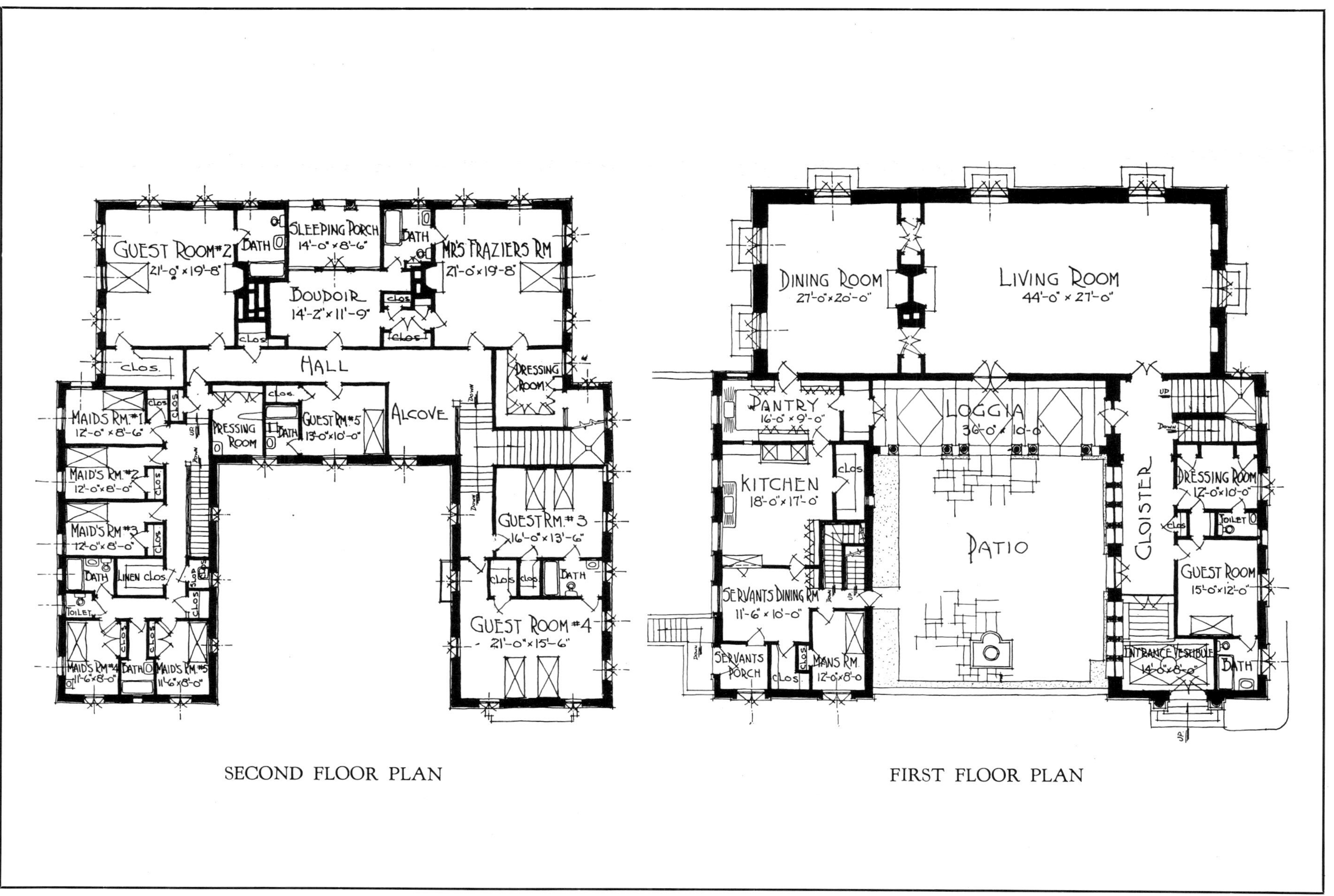

SECOND FLOOR PLAN

FIRST FLOOR PLAN

RESIDENCE FOR MRS. FRANK P. FRAZIER, PALM BEACH, FLORIDA

MARION SIMS WYETH, ARCHITECT

LOGGIA

RESIDENCE FOR MRS. FRANK P. FRAZIER, PALM BEACH, FLORIDA

MARION SIMS WYETH, ARCHITECT

CLOISTER

PATIO

RESIDENCE FOR MRS. FRANK P. FRAZIER, PALM BEACH, FLORIDA

MARION SIMS WYETH, ARCHITECT

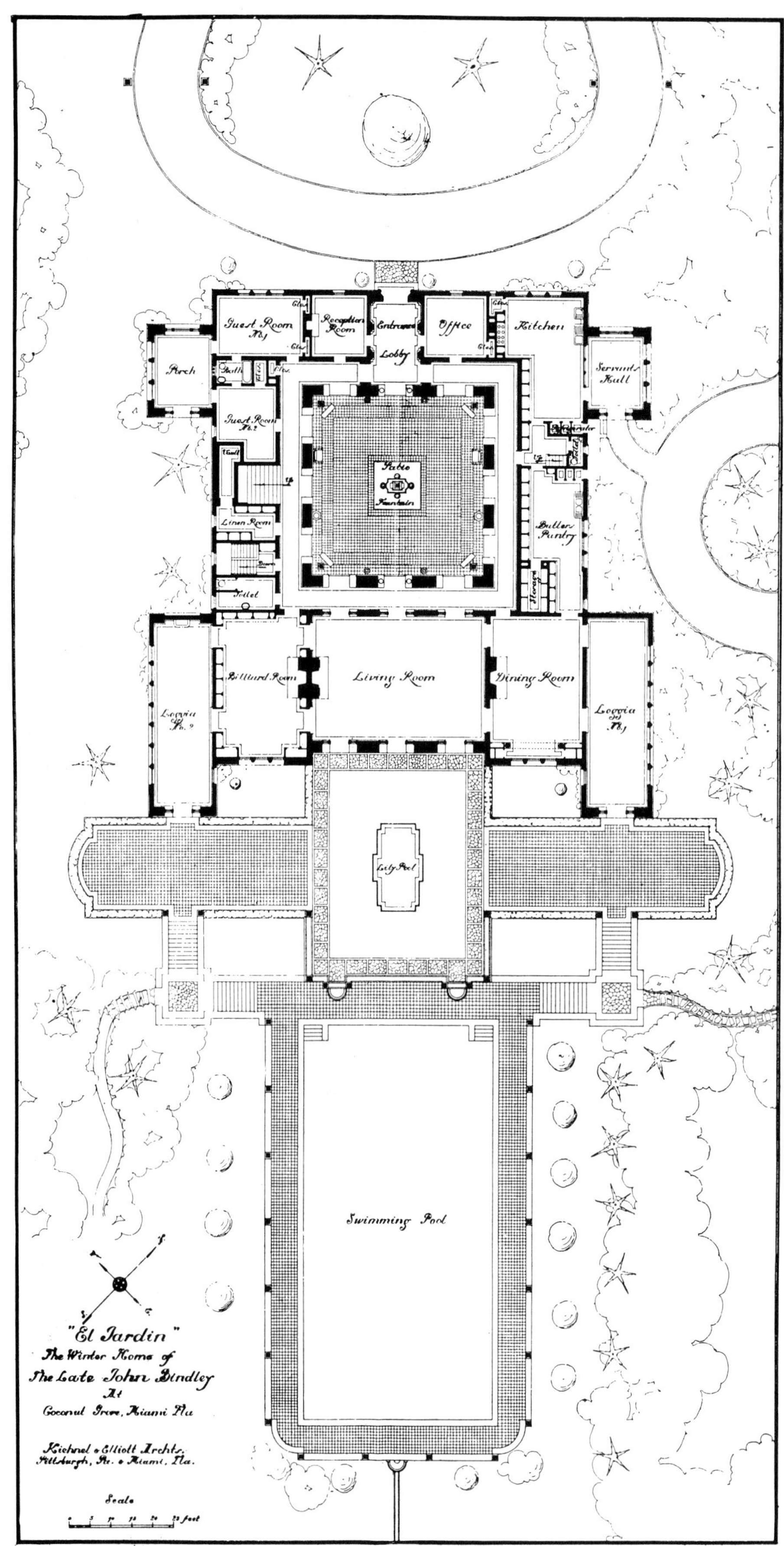

PLAN, "EL JARDIN"

ESTATE OF THE LATE JOHN BINDLEY, COCONUT GROVE, FLORIDA, NOW OWNED BY MR. A. J. RICHEY

KIEHNEL & ELLIOTT, ARCHITECTS

EAST FRONT

"EL JARDIN" ESTATE OF THE LATE JOHN BINDLEY, COCONUT GROVE, FLORIDA, NOW OWNED BY MR. A. J. RICHEY

KIEHNEL & ELLIOTT, ARCHITECTS

ENTRANCE, WEST FACADE

"EL JARDIN" ESTATE OF THE LATE JOHN BINDLEY, COCONUT GROVE, FLORIDA, NOW OWNED BY MR. A. J. RICHEY

KIEHNEL & ELLIOTT, ARCHITECTS

GATE LODGE

GARDEN, PROPAGATION HOUSE OF SLATS

"EL JARDIN" ESTATE OF THE LATE JOHN BINDLEY, COCONUT GROVE, FLORIDA, NOW OWNED BY MR. A. J. RICHEY

KIEHNEL & ELLIOTT, ARCHITECTS

Roof
Gallery
Bed Room
Bed Room
Bed Room
Clos
Trunk Room
Bath
Stair Hall
Hall
Hall
Bed Room
Bed Room
Bed Room
Bath
Bath
Loggia
Residence for
John B Semple Esq
Coconut Grove Fla
Kiehnel and Elliott Archts
Pittsburgh Pa
and
Miami Fla
Second Floor Plan

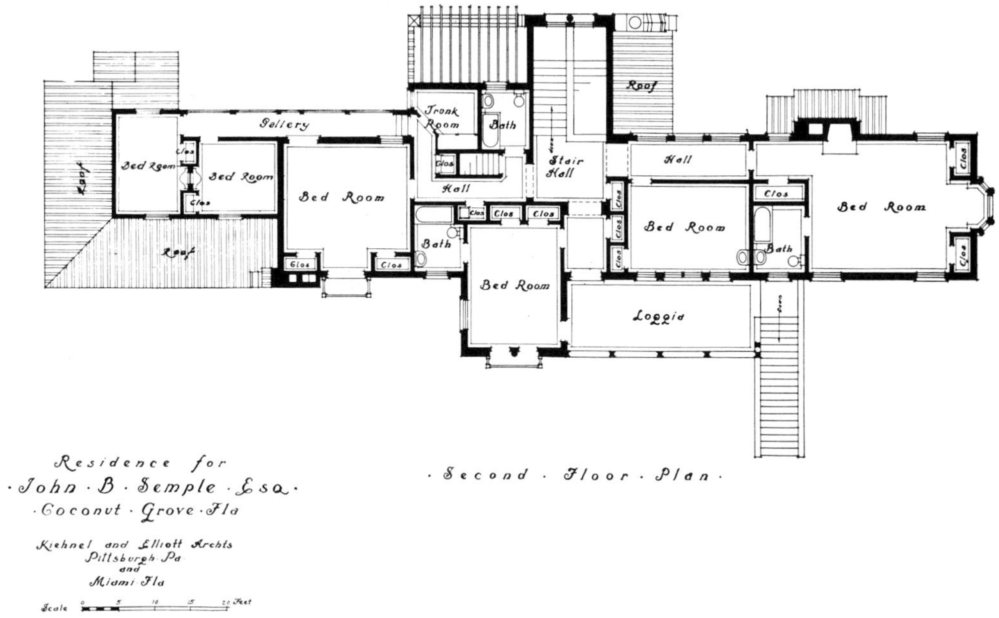

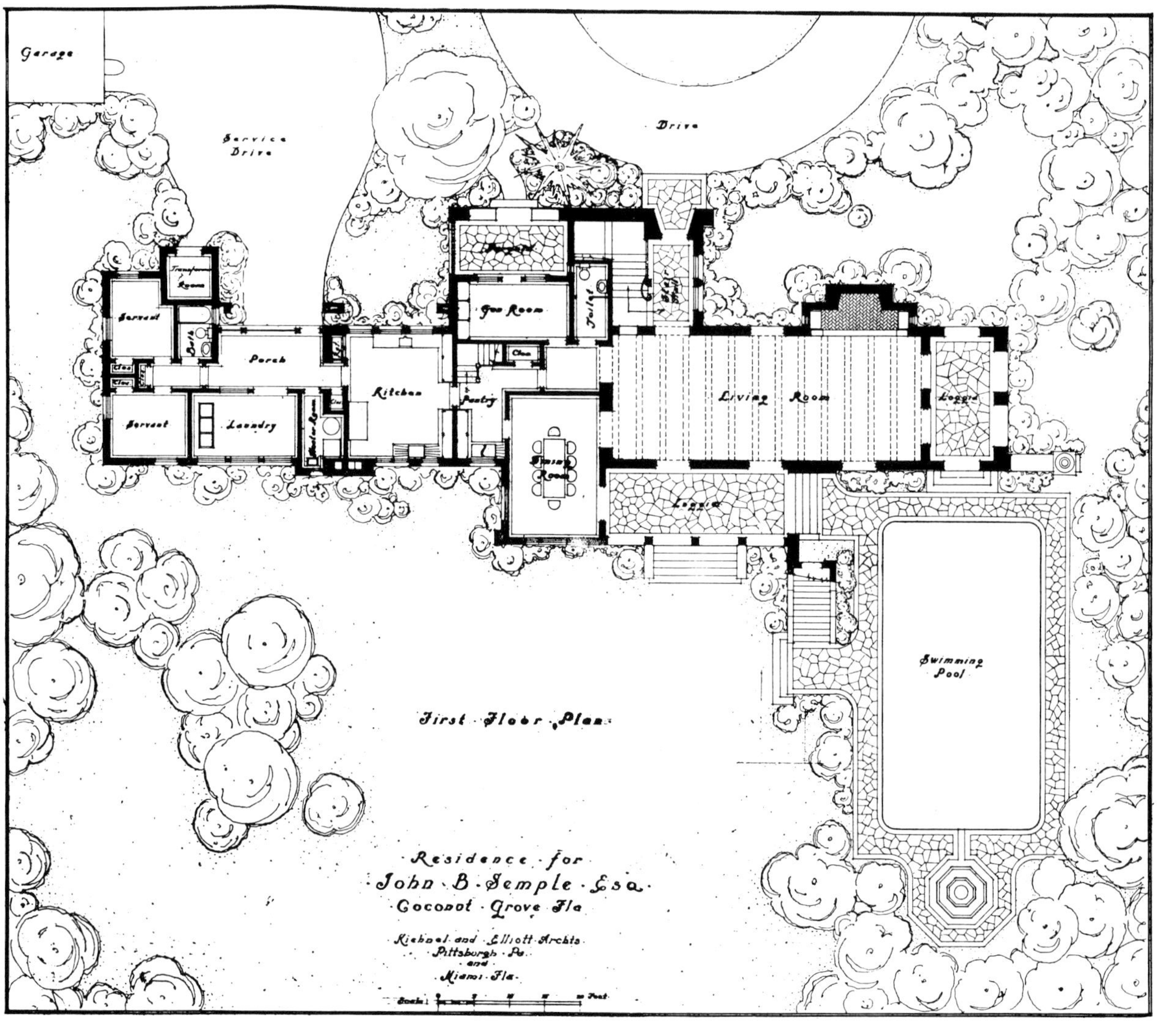

Garage
Service Drive
Drive
Servant
Bath
Porch
Servant
Laundry
Kitchen
Pantry
Gun Room
Toilet
Dining Room
Living Room
Loggia
Loggia
Swimming Pool
First Floor Plan
Residence for
John B Semple Esq
Coconut Grove Fla
Kiehnel and Elliott Archts
Pittsburgh Pa
and
Miami Fla

"LA BRISA", WINTER RESIDENCE FOR MR. JOHN B. SEMPLE,
COCONUT GROVE, FLORIDA

KIEHNEL & ELLIOTT, ARCHITECTS

GENERAL VIEW

"LA BRISA", WINTER RESIDENCE FOR MR. JOHN B. SEMPLE, COCONUT GROVE, FLORIDA

KIEHNEL & ELLIOTT, ARCHITECTS

GARDEN FRONT

"LA BRISA", WINTER RESIDENCE FOR MR. JOHN B. SEMPLE, COCONUT GROVE, FLORIDA

KIEHNEL & ELLIOTT, ARCHITECTS

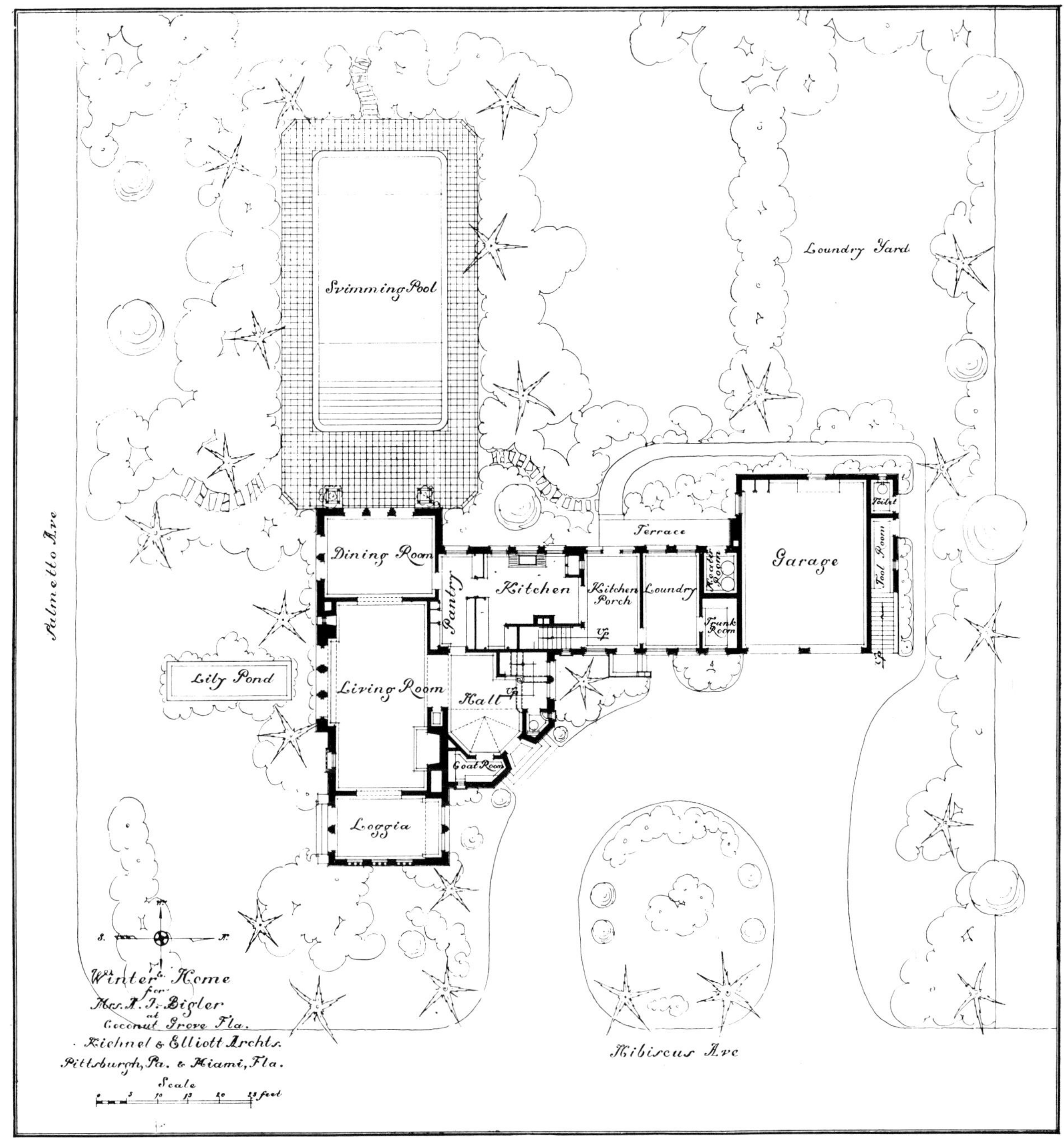

PLAN

RESIDENCE FOR MR. ALBERT BIGLER, COCONUT GROVE, FLORIDA

KIEHNEL & ELLIOTT, ARCHITECTS

ENTRANCE DETAIL

GARDEN FRONT AND POOL, DETAIL

RESIDENCE FOR MR. ALBERT BIGLER, COCONUT GROVE, FLORIDA

KIEHNEL & ELLIOTT, ARCHITECTS

GARDEN FRONT RESIDENCE FOR MR. E. B. DOUGLAS, MIAMI, FLORIDA

KIEHNEL & ELLIOTT, ARCHITECTS

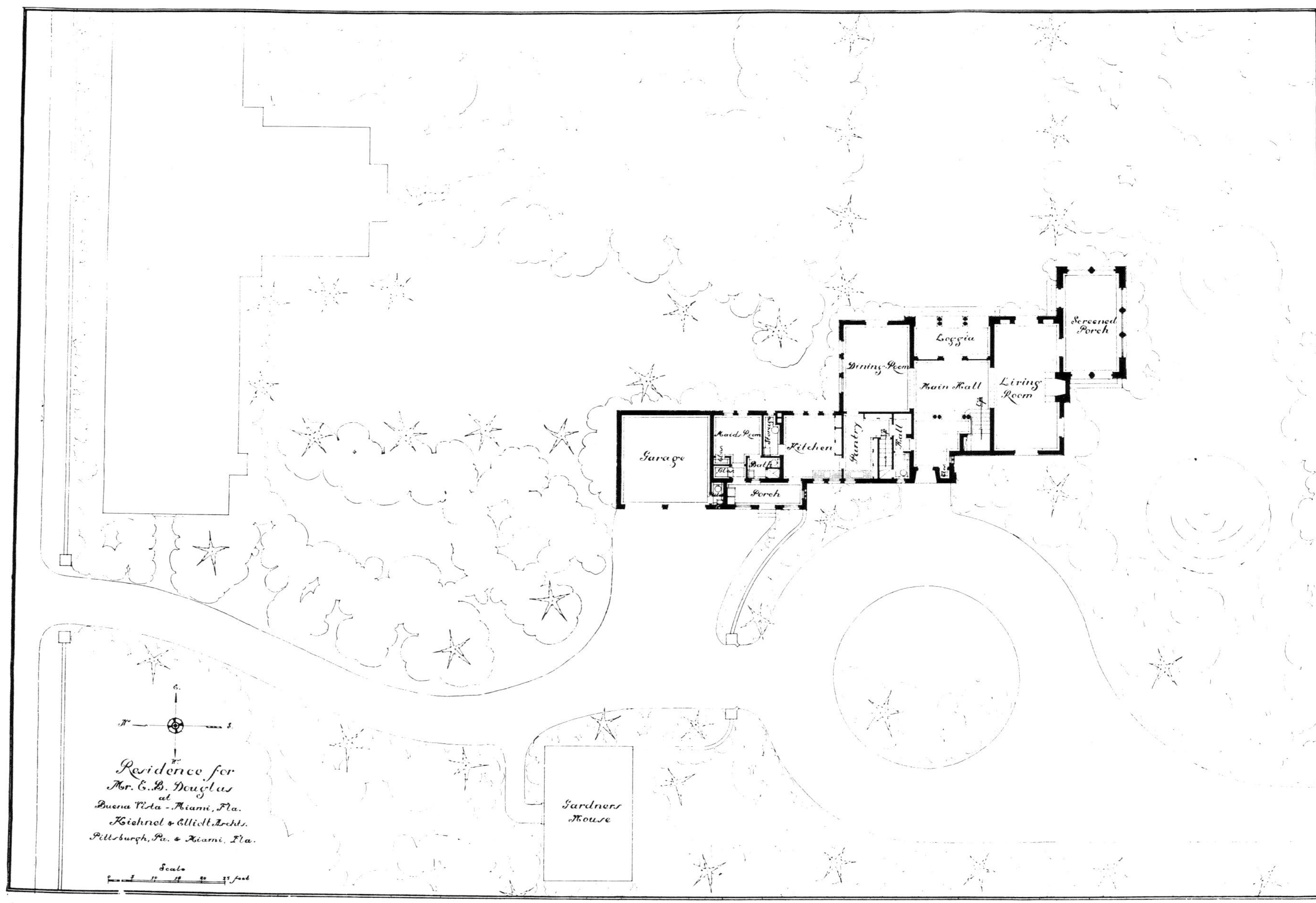

PLAN RESIDENCE FOR MR. E. B. DOUGLAS, MIAMI, FLORIDA
KIEHNEL & ELLIOTT, ARCHITECTS

ENTRANCE FRONT

RESIDENCE FOR MR. E. B. DOUGLAS, MIAMI, FLORIDA

KIEHNEL & ELLIOTT, ARCHITECTS

GENERAL VIEW

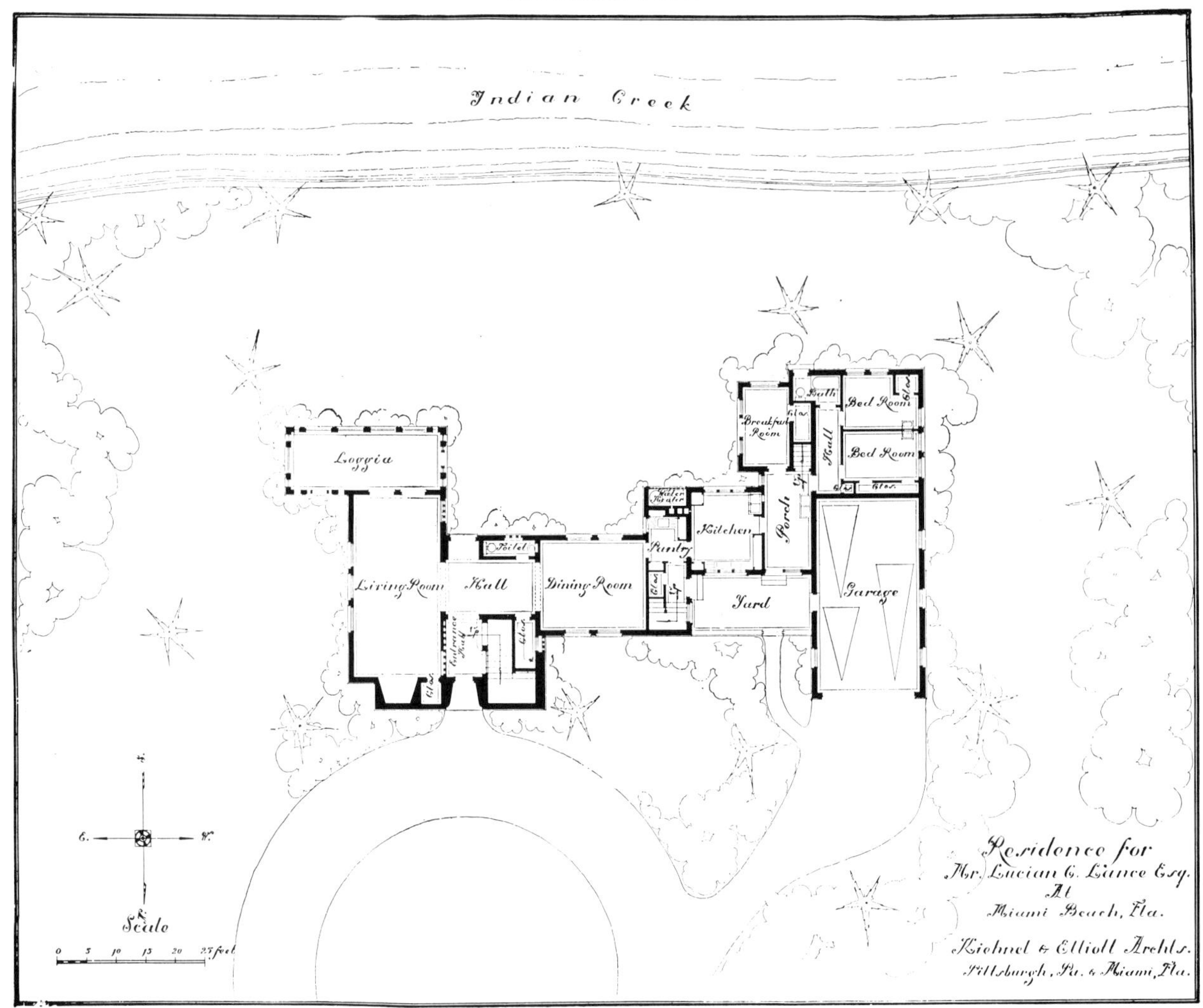

PLAN

RESIDENCE FOR MR. LUCIAN C. LANCE, MIAMI, FLORIDA

KIEHNEL & ELLIOTT, ARCHITECTS

VIEW FROM THE STREET

RESIDENCE FOR MR. THOMAS E. HOGG, OAKMONT, SAN ANTONIO, TEXAS

ATLEE B. AND ROBERT M. AYRES, ARCHITECTS

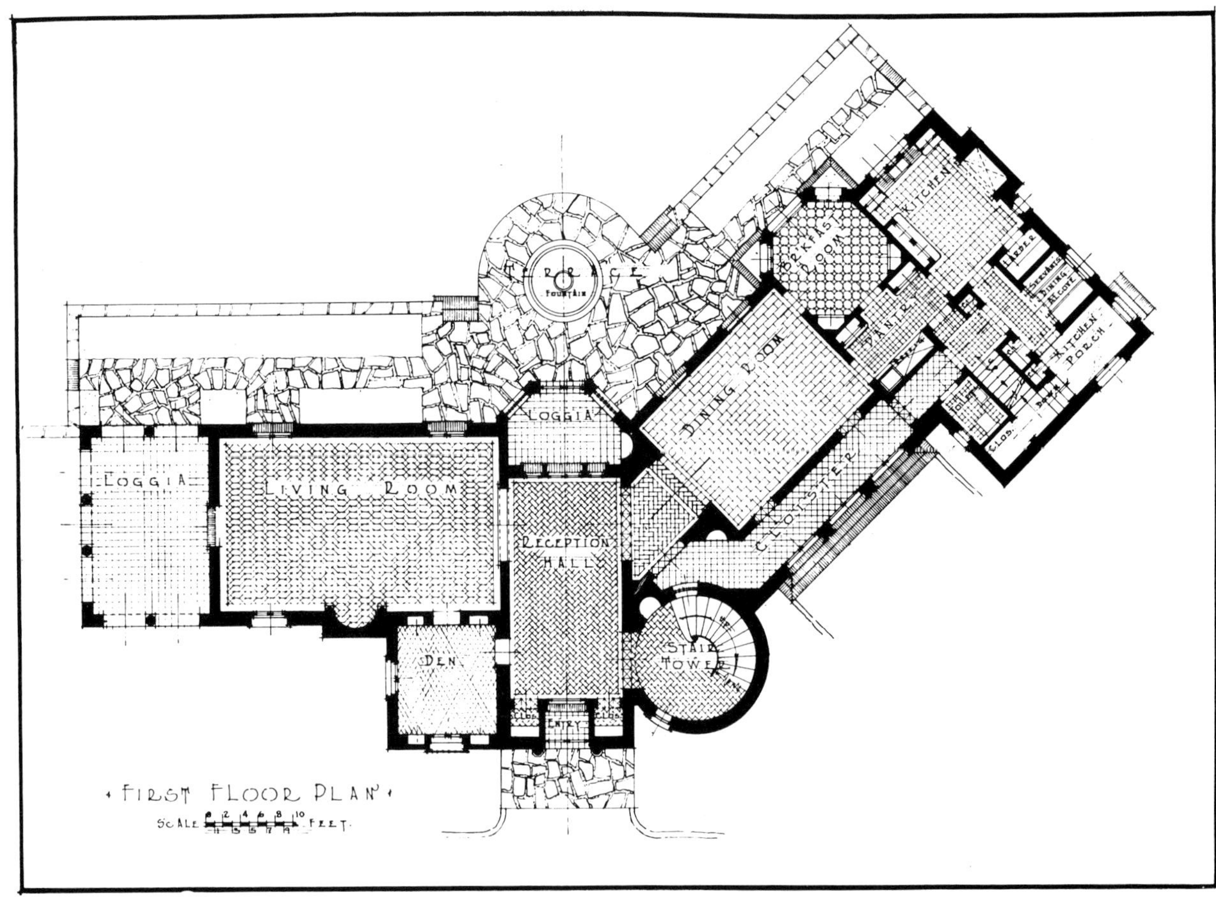

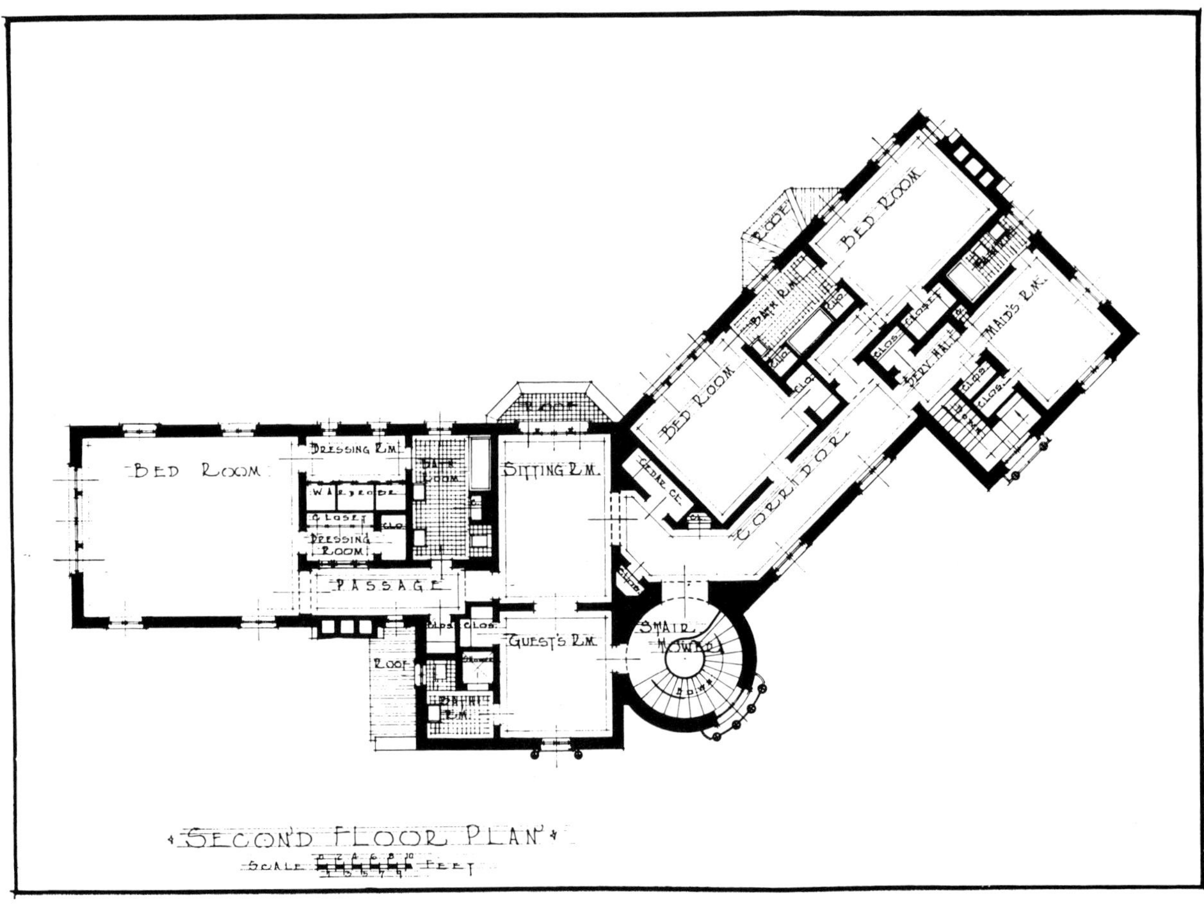

RESIDENCE FOR THOMAS E. HOGG, OAKMONT, SAN ANTONIO, TEXAS

ATLEE B. AND ROBERT M. AYRES, ARCHITECTS

TOWER FROM GARDEN GATE

REAR LOGGIA

RESIDENCE FOR MR. THOMAS E. HOGG, OAKMONT, SAN ANTONIO, TEXAS

ATLEE B. AND ROBERT M. AYRES, ARCHITECTS

STAIRCASE

ENTRY

RESIDENCE FOR MR. THOMAS E. HOGG, OAKMONT, SAN ANTONIO, TEXAS

ATLEE B. AND ROBERT M. AYRES, ARCHITECTS

FRONT ELEVATION

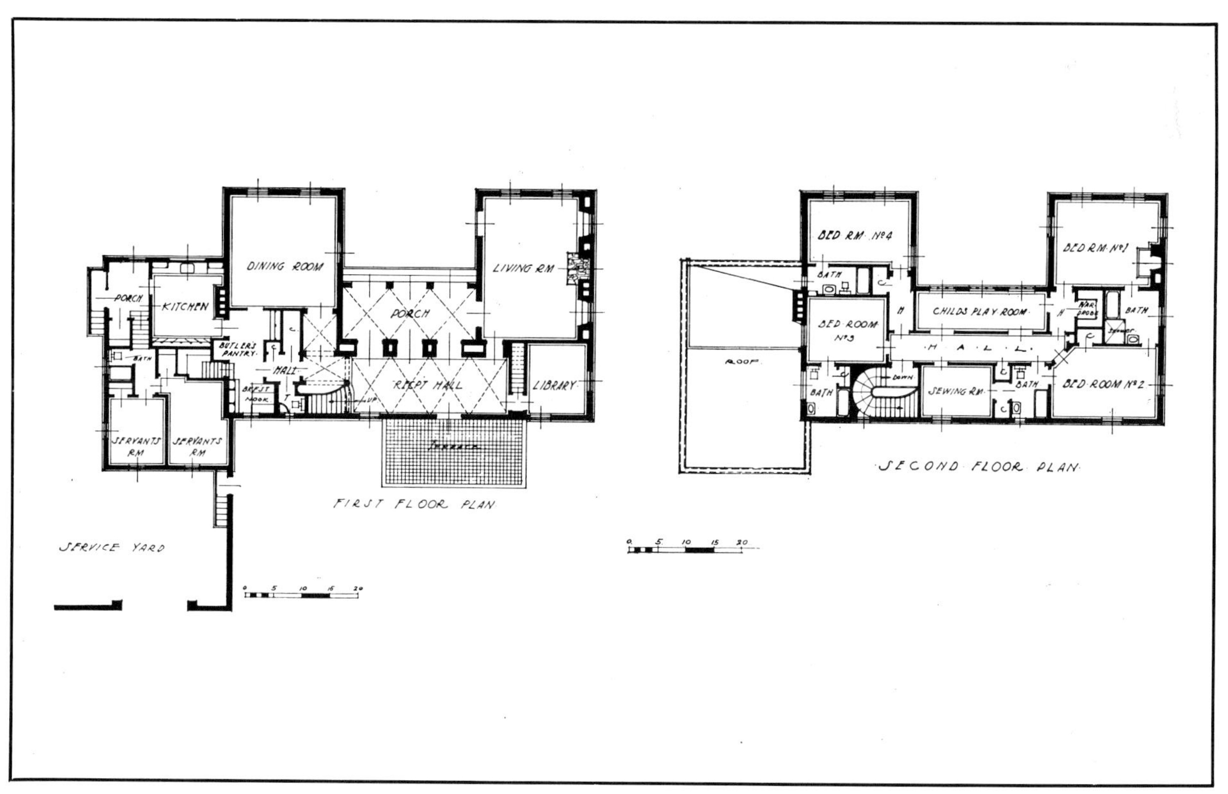

RESIDENCE FOR MR. M. D. ARNOLD, JR., KNOXVILLE, TENNESSEE

BARBER & McMURRY, ARCHITECTS

FRONT ELEVATION

TERRACE FACADE

RESIDENCE FOR MR. W. W. KELLY, CLEVELAND, OHIO

CHARLES S. SCHNEIDER, ARCHITECT

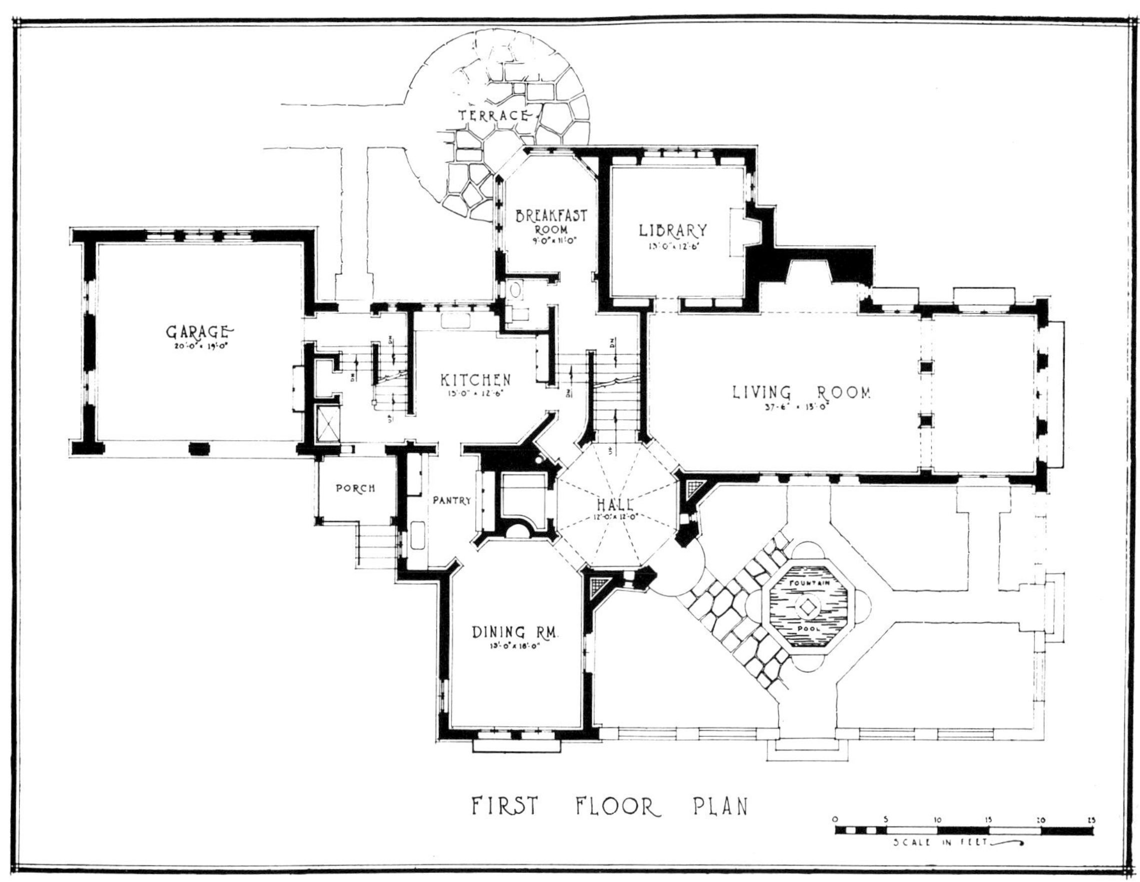

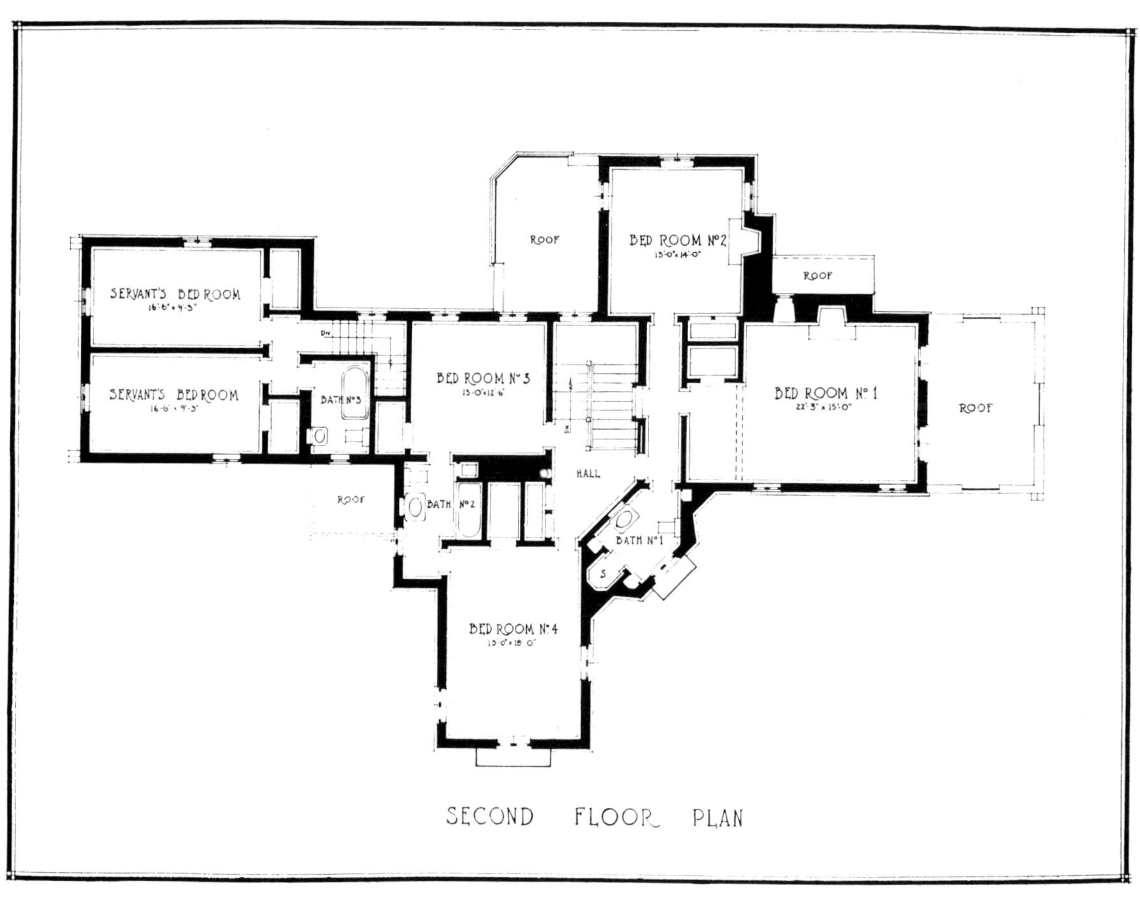

RESIDENCE FOR MR. W. W. KELLY, CLEVELAND, OHIO

CHARLES S. SCHNEIDER, ARCHITECT

MAIN ENTRANCE AND TERRACE

RESIDENCE FOR MR. W. W. KELLY, CLEVELAND, OHIO

CHARLES S. SCHNEIDER, ARCHITECT

LIVING ROOM DETAIL

FIREPLACE IN LIVING ROOM

RESIDENCE FOR MR. W. W. KELLY, CLEVELAND, OHIO

CHARLES S. SCHNEIDER, ARCHITECT

GARDEN ELEVATION RESIDENCE FOR MR. IRVIN F. LEHMAN, PITTSBURGH, PENNSYLVANIA

THEODORE EICHHOLZ, ARCHITECT

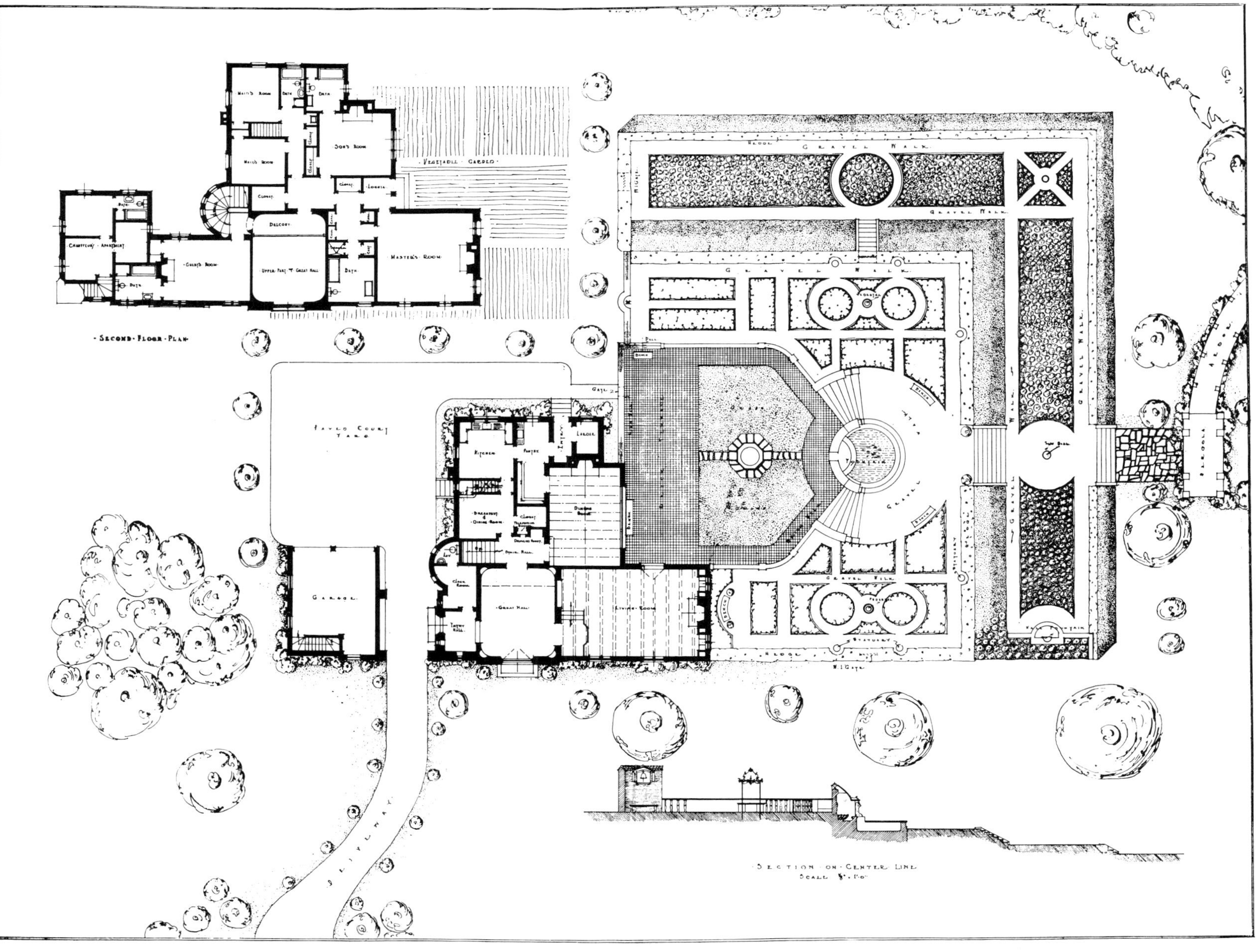

RESIDENCE FOR MR. IRVIN F. LEHMAN, PITTSBURGH, PENNSYLVANIA
THEODORE EICHHOLZ, ARCHITECT

GREAT HALL

RESIDENCE FOR MR. IRVIN F. LEHMAN, PITTSBURGH, PENNSYLVANIA

THEODORE EICHHOLZ, ARCHITECT

LIVING ROOM

LIVING ROOM

RESIDENCE FOR MR. IRVIN F. LEHMAN, PITTSBURGH, PENNSYLVANIA

THEODORE EICHHOLZ, ARCHITECT

DINING ROOM RESIDENCE FOR MR. IRVIN F. LEHMAN, PITTSBURGH, PENNSYLVANIA

THEODORE EICHHOLZ, ARCHITECT

GENERAL VIEW RESIDENCE FOR MR. W. O. VAN ARSDALE, WICHITA, KANSAS
LORENTZ SCHMIDT & CO., ARCHITECTS

VIEW FROM LOGGIA

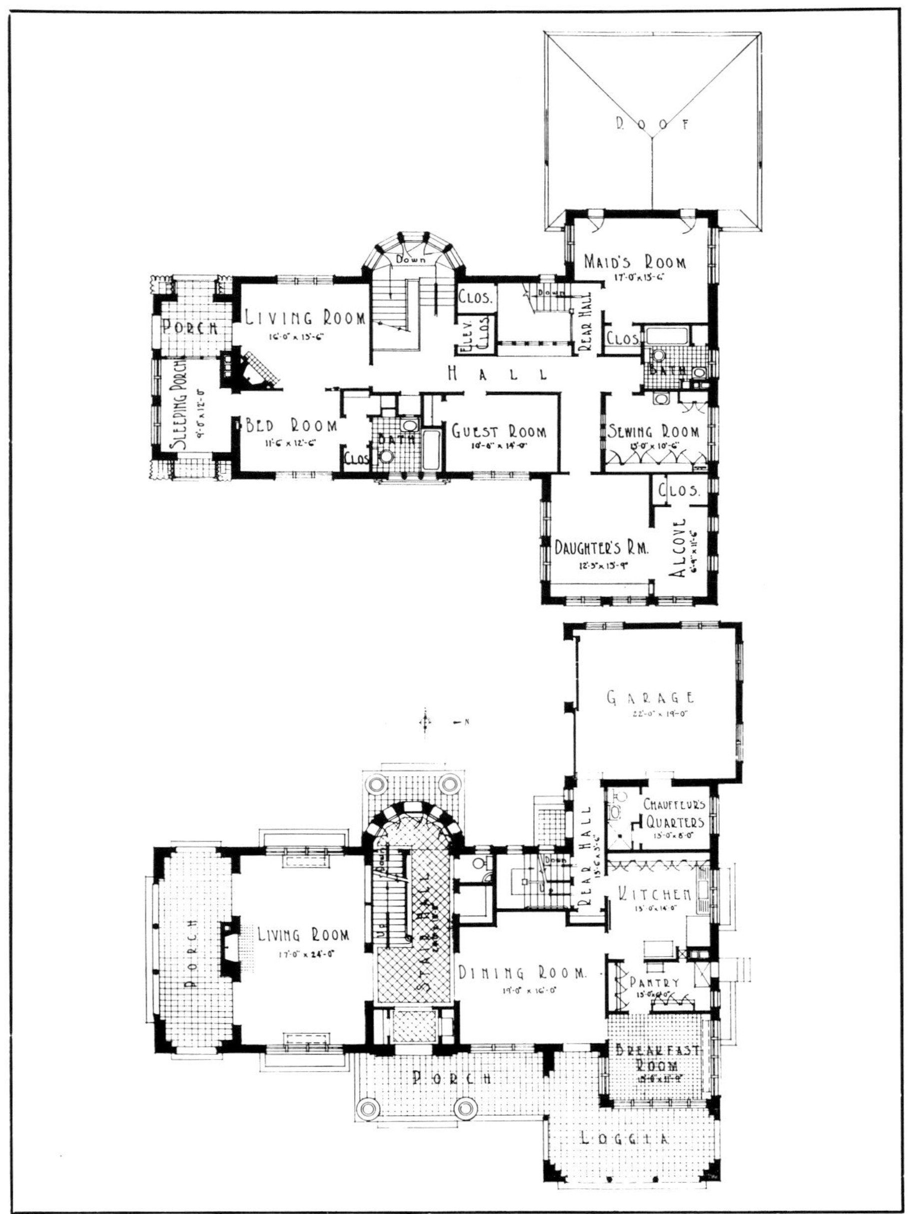

PLANS

RESIDENCE FOR MR. W. O. VAN ARSDALE, WICHITA, KANSAS

LORENTZ SCHMIDT & CO., ARCHITECTS

GENERAL VIEW RESIDENCE FOR MRS. WM. LESLIE WELTON, BIRMINGHAM, ALABAMA

WM. LESLIE WELTON, ARCHITECT

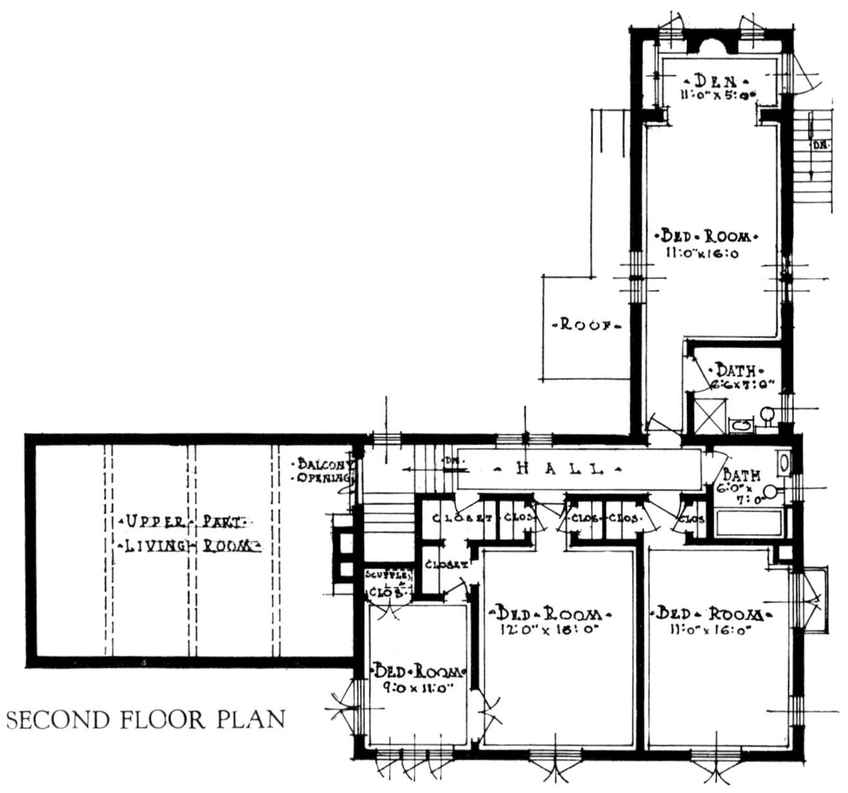

SECOND FLOOR PLAN

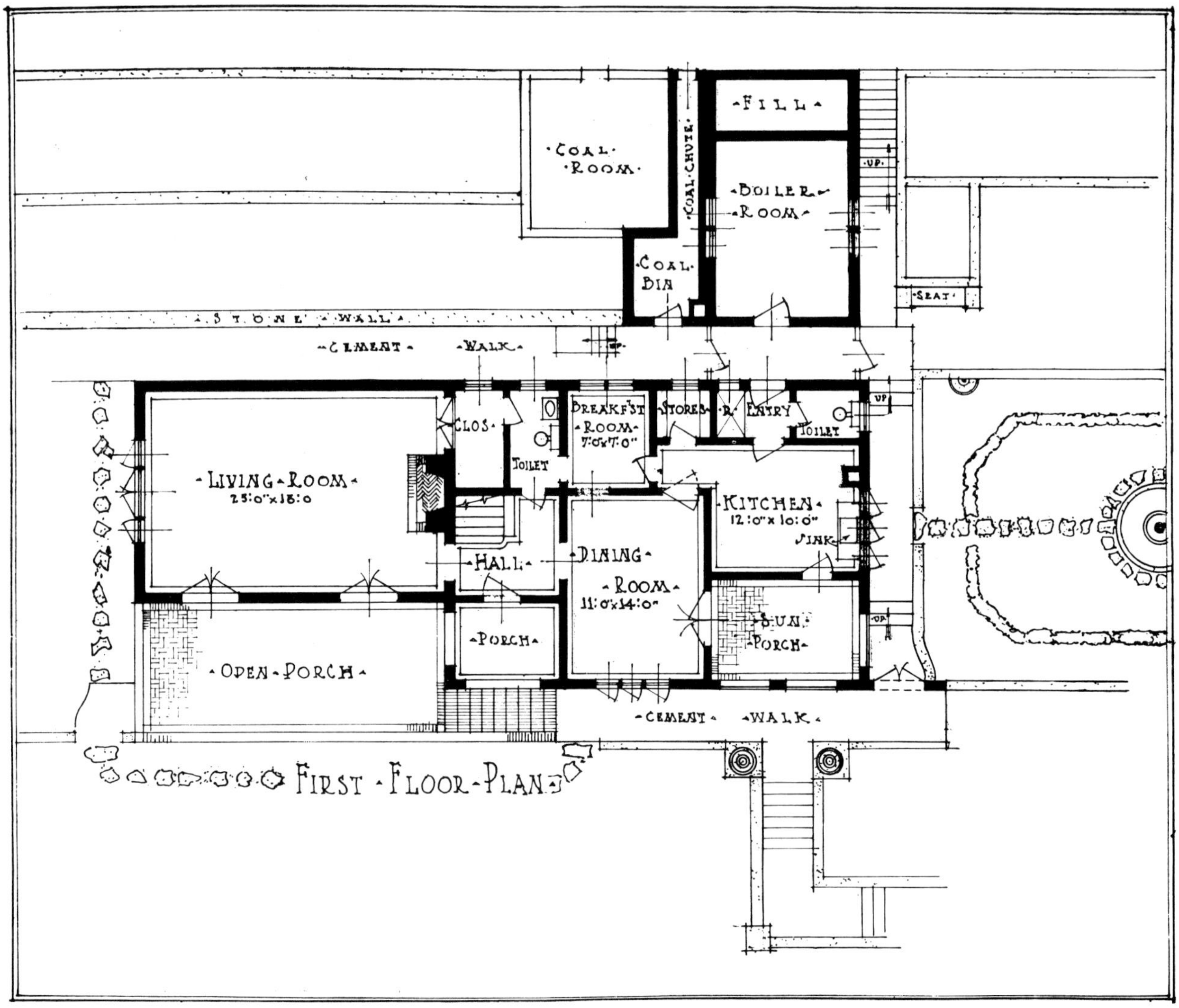

FILL
COAL ROOM
COAL CHUTE
BOILER ROOM
COAL BIN
SEAT
STONE WALL
CEMENT WALK
CLOS
TOILET
BREAKF'ST ROOM
7:0"x7:0"
STORES
ENTRY
TOILET
LIVING ROOM
25:0"x18:0
KITCHEN
12:0"x 10:0"
SINK
HALL
DINING ROOM
11:0"x14:0"
SUN PORCH
PORCH
OPEN PORCH
CEMENT WALK
FIRST FLOOR PLAN

RESIDENCE FOR MRS. WM. LESLIE WELTON, BIRMINGHAM, ALABAMA

WM. LESLIE WELTON, ARCHITECT

GARDEN FOR MR. DOUGLAS SMITH, ALTADENA, CALIFORNIA
FLORENCE YOCK, LANDSCAPE ARCHITECT

GENERAL VIEW

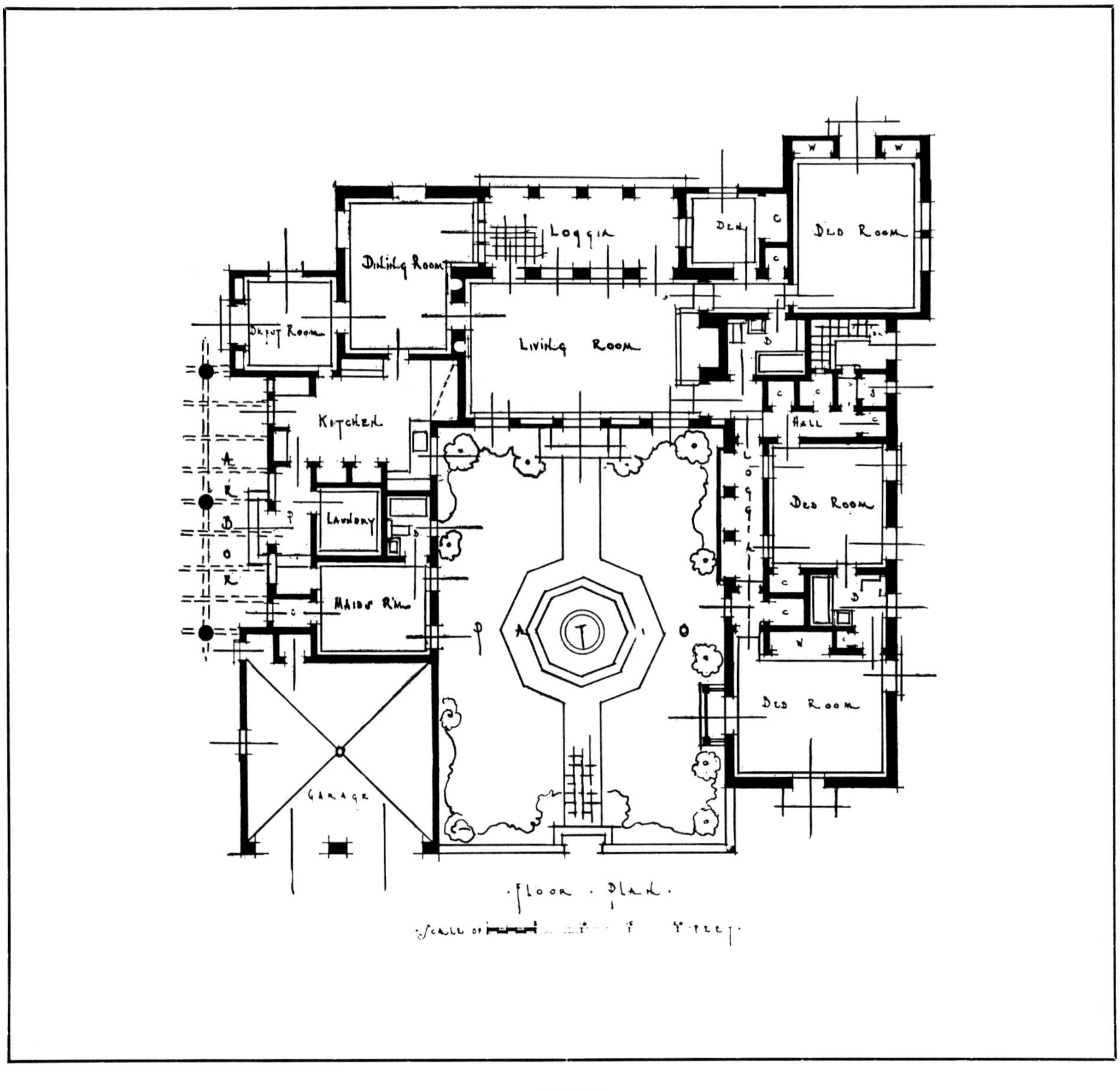

PLAN

RESIDENCE FOR MR. ROY B. WILTSIE, LA JOLLA, CALIFORNIA

EDGAR V. ULLRICH, ARCHITECT

FRONT FACADE

RESIDENCE FOR MR. ROY B. WILTSIE, LA JOLLA, CALIFORNIA

EDGAR V. ULLRICH, ARCHITECT

DOORWAY

RESIDENCE FOR MR. ROY B. WILTSIE, LA JOLLA, CALIFORNIA
EDGAR V. ULLRICH, ARCHITECT

OCEAN FRONT, LOGGIA

PATIO

RESIDENCE FOR MR. ROY B. WILTSIE, LA JOLLA, CALIFORNIA

EDGAR V. ULLRICH, ARCHITECT

FRONT ELEVATION WITH VIEW OF THE SEA

SOUTH WEST FRONT

RESIDENCE FOR MR. FRANK TURNBULL, LA JOLLA, CALIFORNIA

EDGAR V. ULLRICH, ARCHITECT

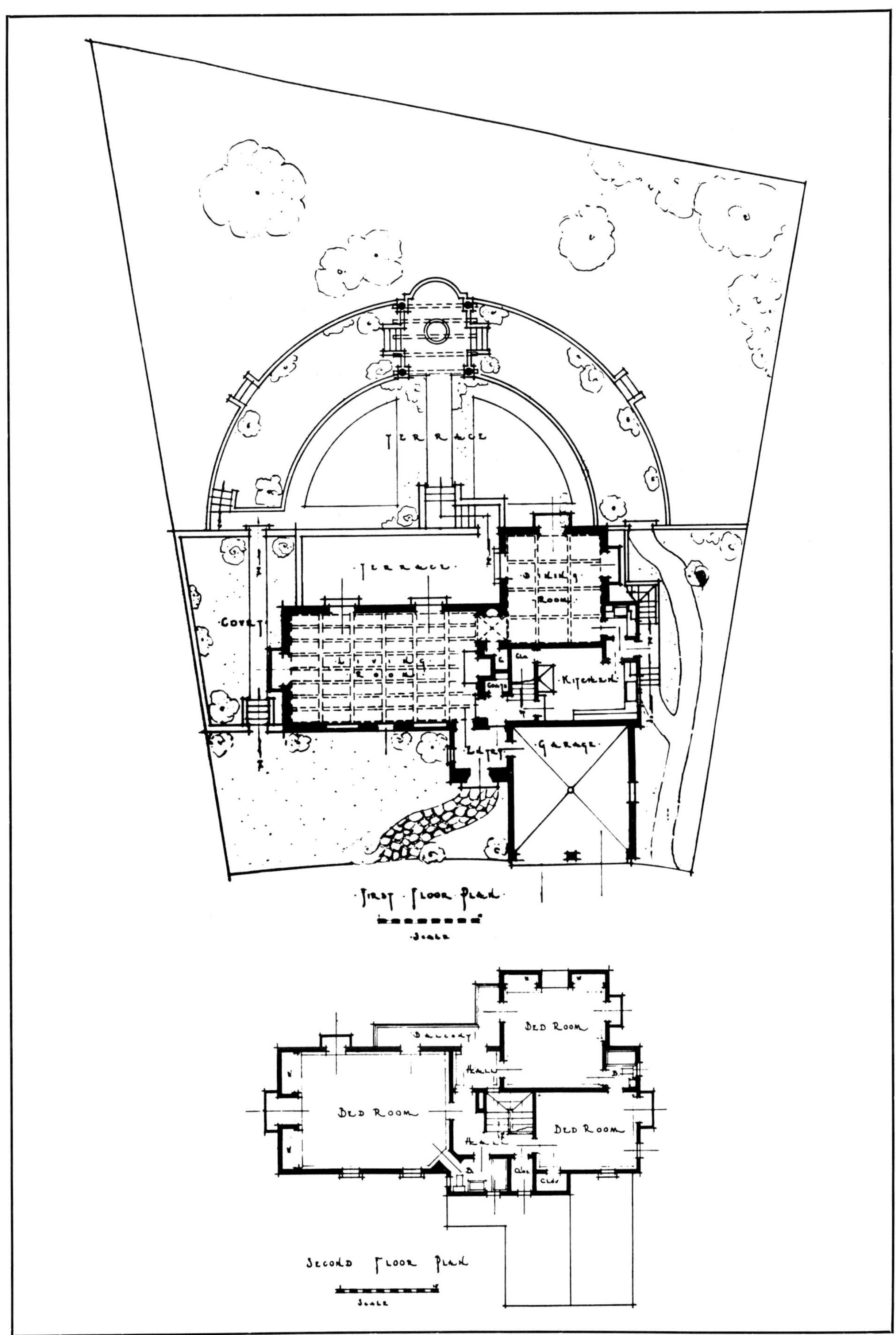

RESIDENCE FOR MR. FRANK TURNBULL, LA JOLLA, CALIFORNIA
EDGAR V. ULLRICH, ARCHITECT

FACADE

RESIDENCE FOR MR. HENRY W. SCHULTZ,
PASADENA, CALIFORNIA

WALLACE NEFF, ARCHITECT

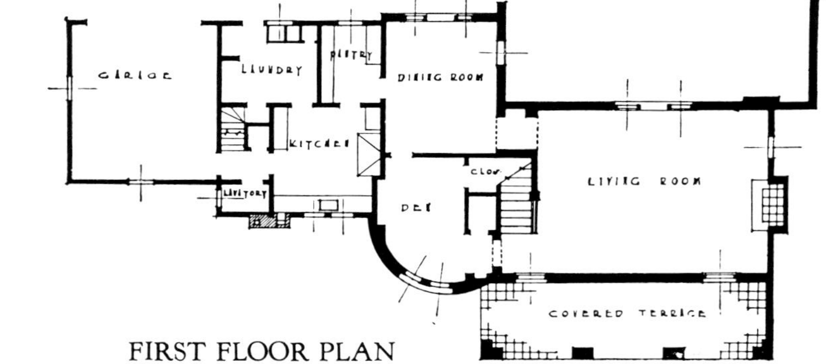

FIRST FLOOR PLAN

DETAIL OF TOWER AND PORCHES

RESIDENCE FOR MR. HENRY W. SCHULTZ, PASADENA, CALIFORNIA

WALLACE NEFF, ARCHITECT

THE GARAGE

THE HOUSE

RESIDENCE FOR DR. GEORGE WATSON COLE, PASADENA, CALIFORNIA

MYRON HUNT, ARCHITECT

VIEW FROM GARDEN RESIDENCE FOR MR. JOHN WILLIS BAER, MONTECITO, CALIFORNIA

WALLACE NEFF, ARCHITECT

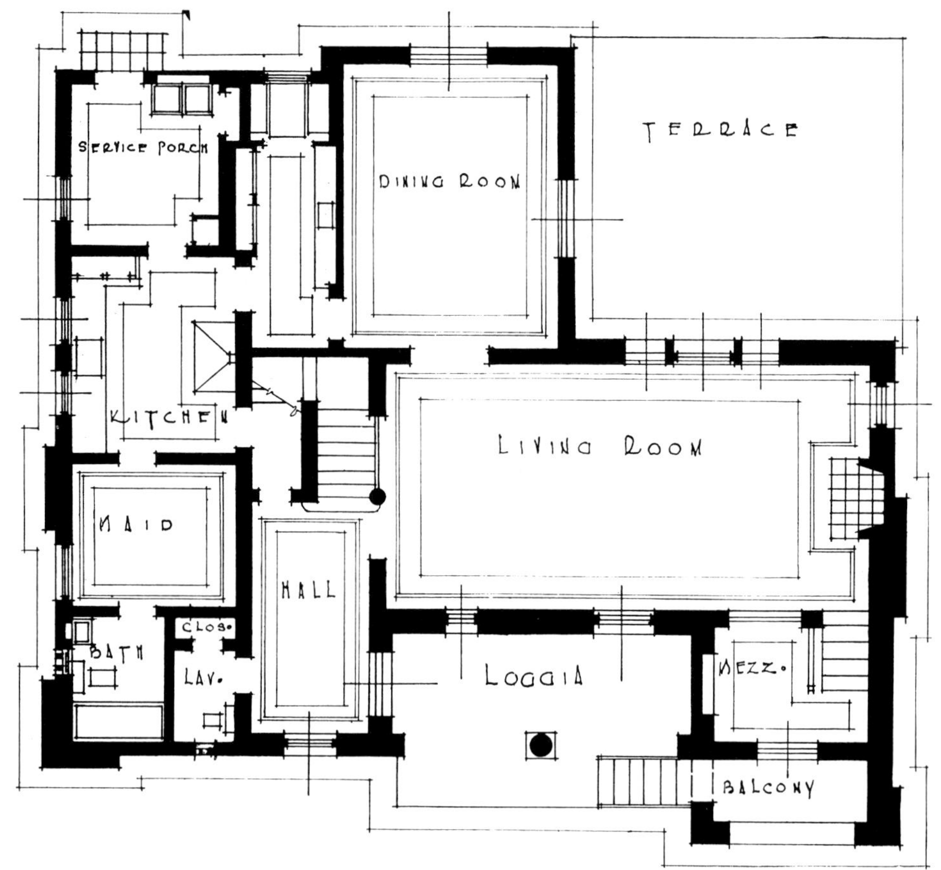

FIRST FLOOR PLAN OF RESIDENCE ON PAGE 185

ENTRANCE STAIRWAY

RESIDENCE FOR MR. PARKER TOMS, PASADENA, CALIFORNIA

WALLACE NEFF, ARCHITECT

GENERAL VIEW RESIDENCE FOR MR. PARKER TOMS, PASADENA, CALIFORNIA

WALLACE NEFF, ARCHITECT

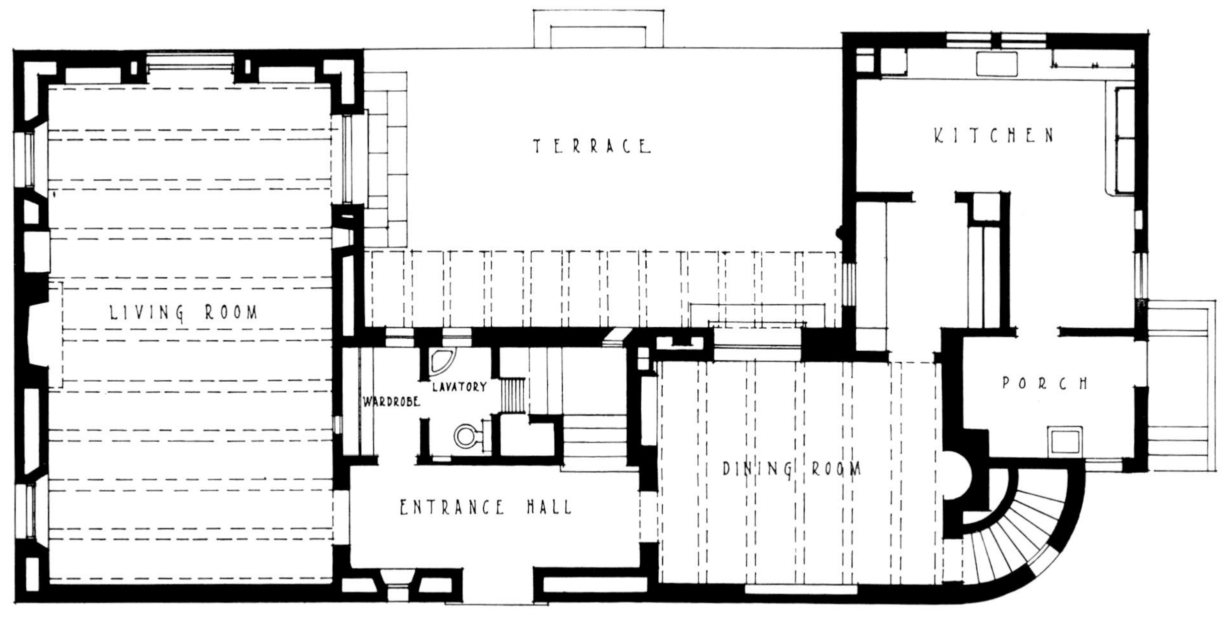

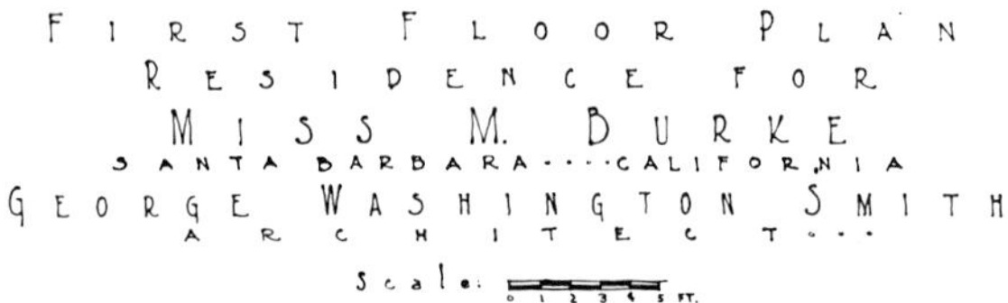

TERRACE FACADE

RESIDENCE FOR MISS MARY BURK, SANTA BARBARA, CALIFORNIA

GEORGE WASHINGTON SMITH, ARCHITECT

TERRACE

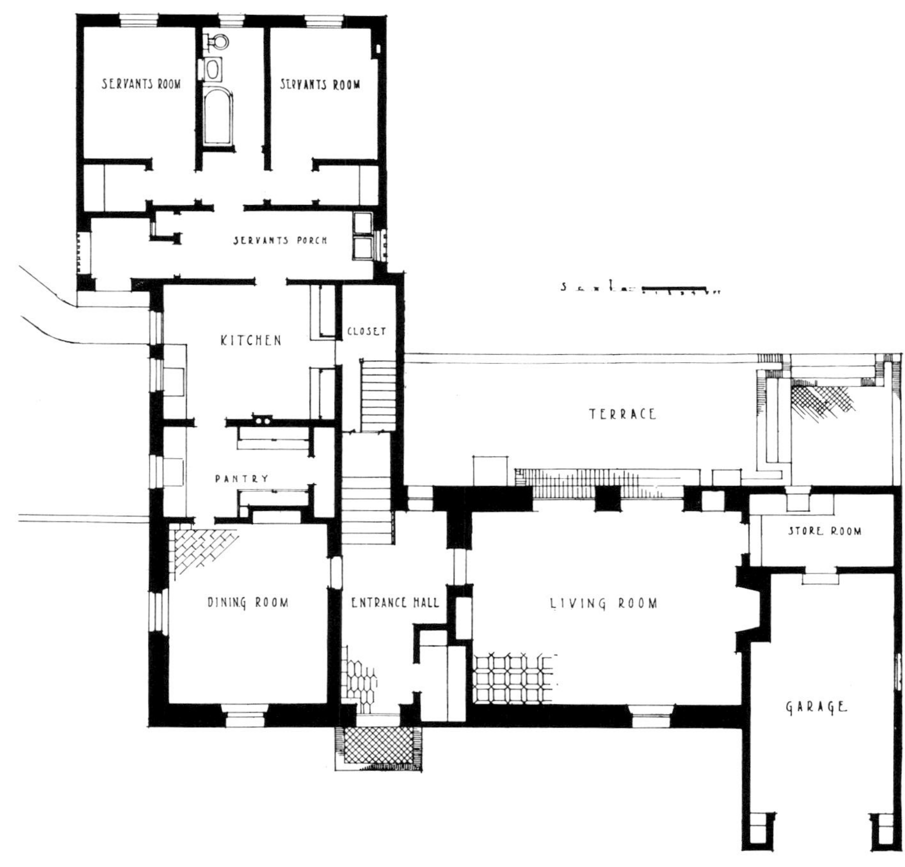

PLAN

RESIDENCE FOR MR. BROOKS FROTHINGHAM, SANTA BARBARA, CALIFORNIA

GEORGE WASHINGTON SMITH, ARCHITECT

FRONT

SIDE ELEVATION

RESIDENCE FOR MR. C. C. STANLEY, PASADENA, CALIFORNIA

MARSTON, VAN PELT & MAYBURY, ARCHITECTS

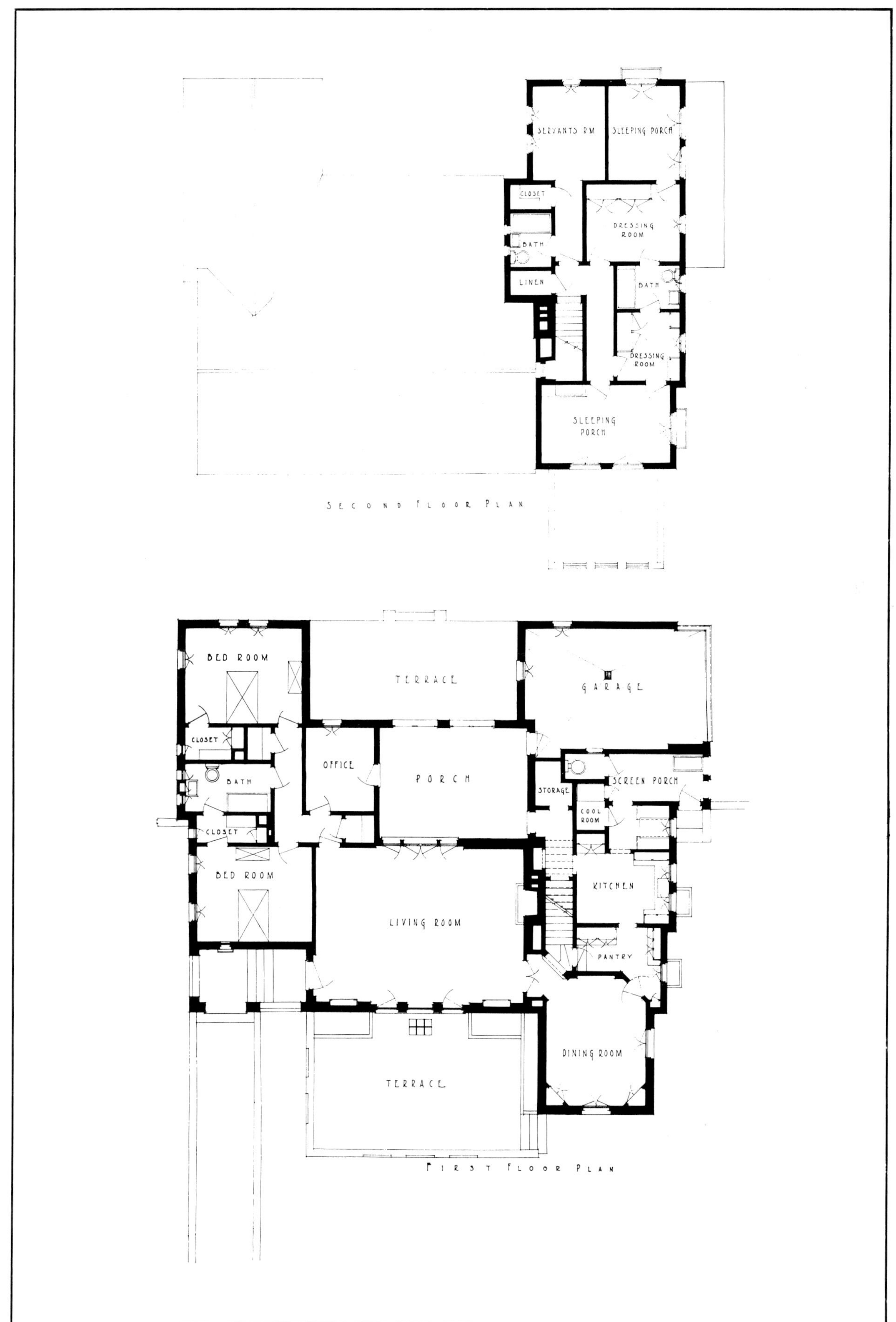

PLANS

RESIDENCE FOR MR. C. C. STANLEY, PASADENA, CALIFORNIA

MARSTON, VAN PELT & MAYBURY, ARCHITECTS

TERRACE

ENTRANCE

RESIDENCE FOR MR. C. C. STANLEY, PASADENA, CALIFORNIA

MARSTON, VAN PELT & MAYBURY, ARCHITECTS

GENERAL VIEW

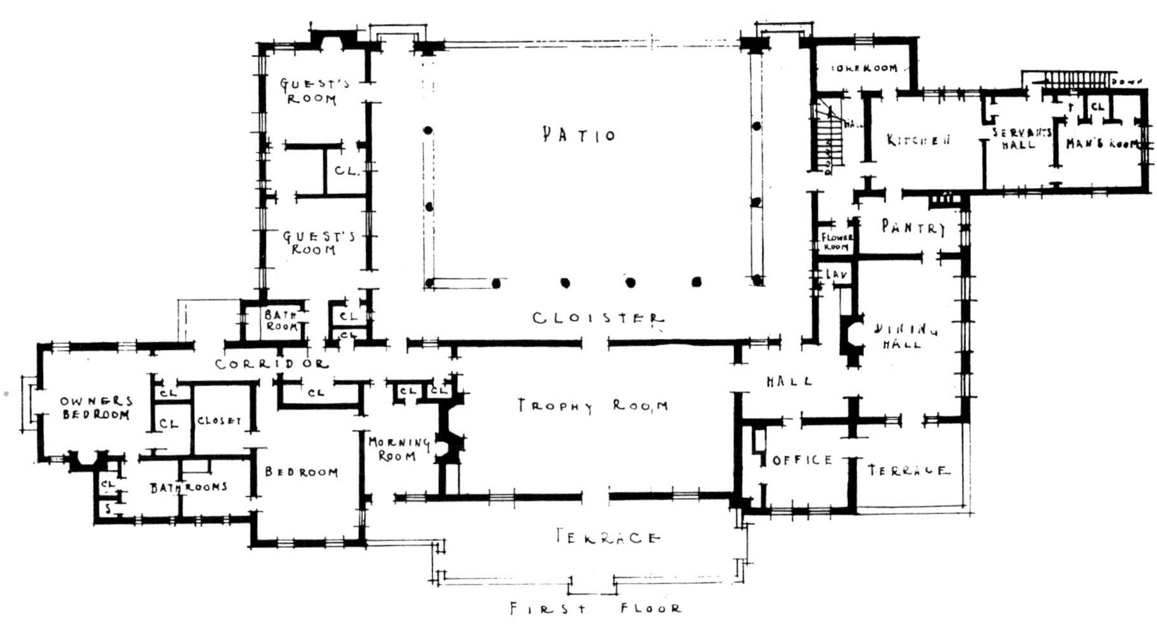

PLAN

RESIDENCE FOR MAJOR MAX FLEISCHMAN, CARPENTERIA, CALIFORNIA

REGINALD D. JOHNSON, ARCHITECT

ENTRANCE

PATIO DETAIL

PATIO

RESIDENCE FOR MAJOR MAX FLEISCHMAN, CARPENTERIA, CALIFORNIA

REGINALD D. JOHNSON, ARCHITECT

GENERAL VIEW

HOUSE, SEA SIDE VIEW

RESIDENCE FOR MR. D. L. JAMES, CARMEL HIGHLANDS, CALIFORNIA

SUMNER C. GREENE, ARCHITECT

HOUSE, LAND SIDE VIEW

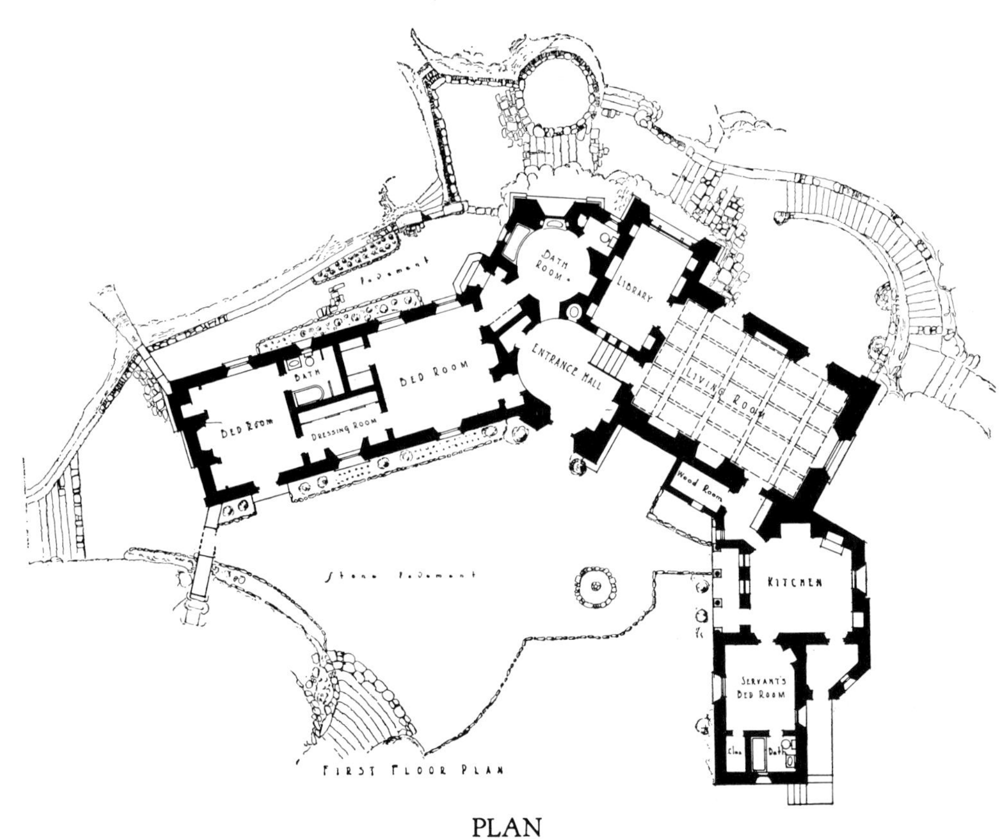

PLAN

RESIDENCE FOR MR. D. L. JAMES, CARMEL HIGHLANDS, CALIFORNIA

SUMNER C. GREENE, ARCHITECT

GENERAL VIEW RESIDENCE FOR MRS. EDITH WYMAN WILSON, MIAMI BEACH, FLORIDA

ROBERT L. WEED, ARCHITECT

PATIO

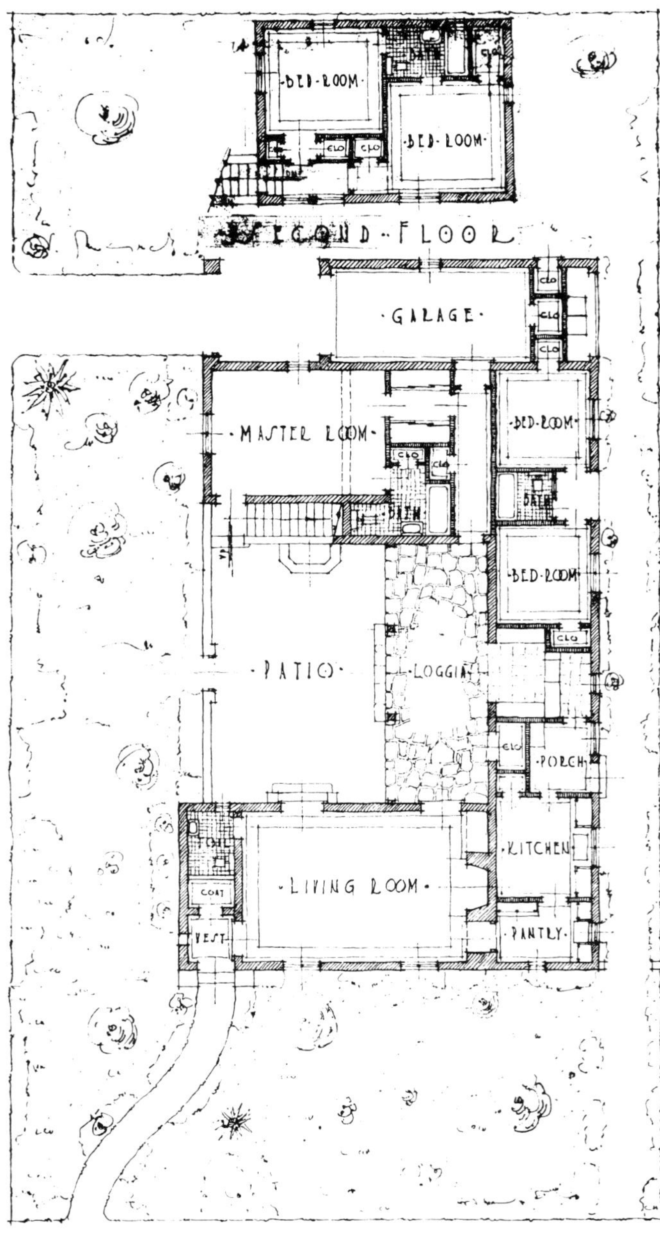

PLAN

RESIDENCE FOR MRS. EDITH WYMAN WILSON, MIAMI BEACH, FLORIDA

ROBERT L. WEED, ARCHITECT

MAIN APPROACH RESIDENCE FOR MR. CHARLES M. EATON, MIAMI BEACH, FLORIDA
ROBERT L. WEED, ARCHITECT

ENTRANCE COURTYARD

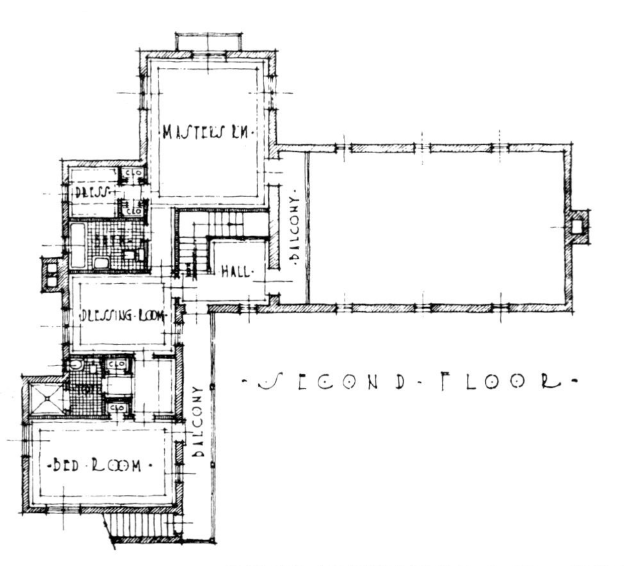

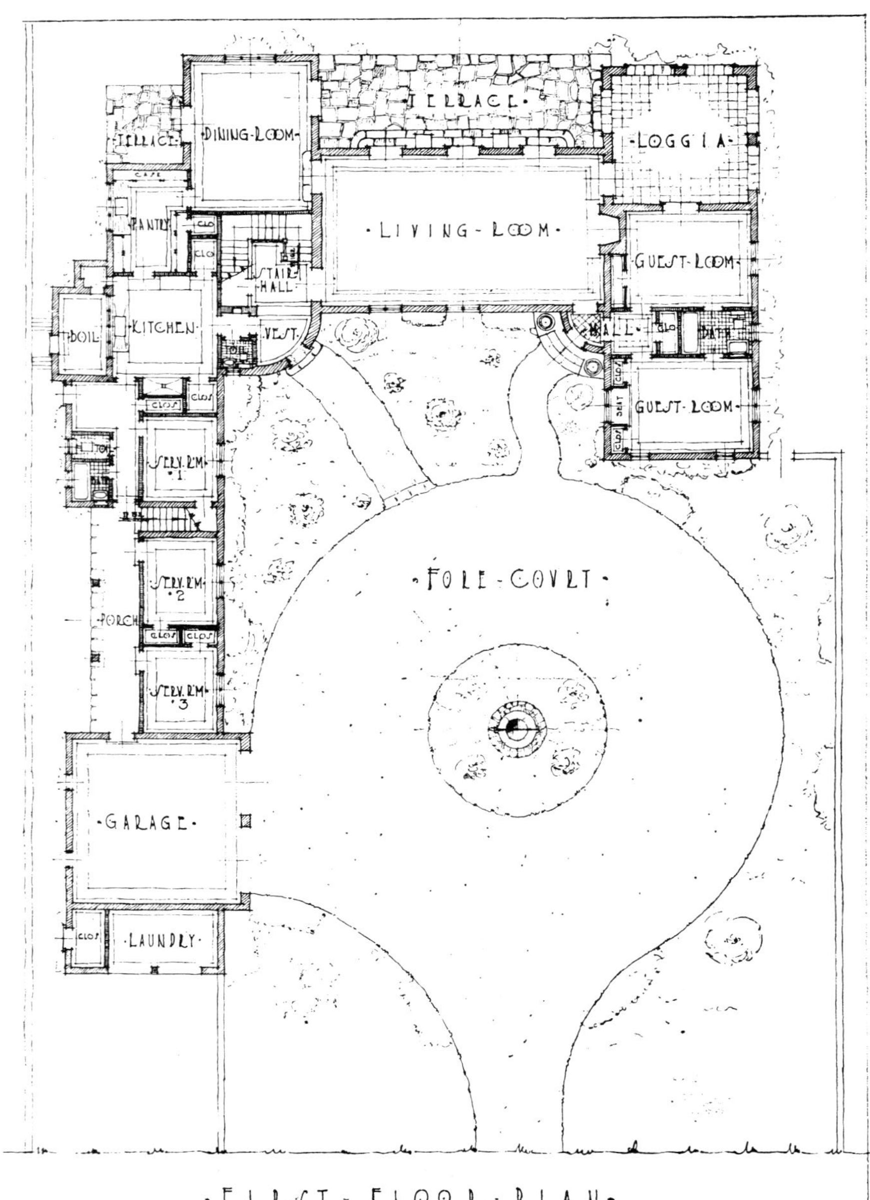

RESIDENCE FOR MR. CHARLES M. EATON, MIAMI BEACH, FLORIDA

ROBERT L. WEED, ARCHITECT

WELL HEAD IN COURTYARD

GUEST WING ENTRANCE

RESIDENCE FOR MR. CHARLES M. EATON, MIAMI BEACH, FLORIDA

ROBERT L. WEED, ARCHITECT

GENERAL VIEW RESIDENCE FOR MR. G. A. MEDCALFE, MIAMI BEACH, FLORIDA

ROBERT L. WEED, ARCHITECT

GARDEN ENTRANCE

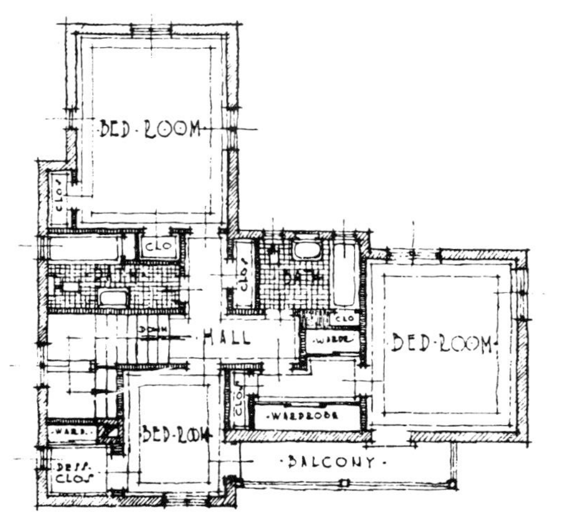

SECOND FLOOR PLAN

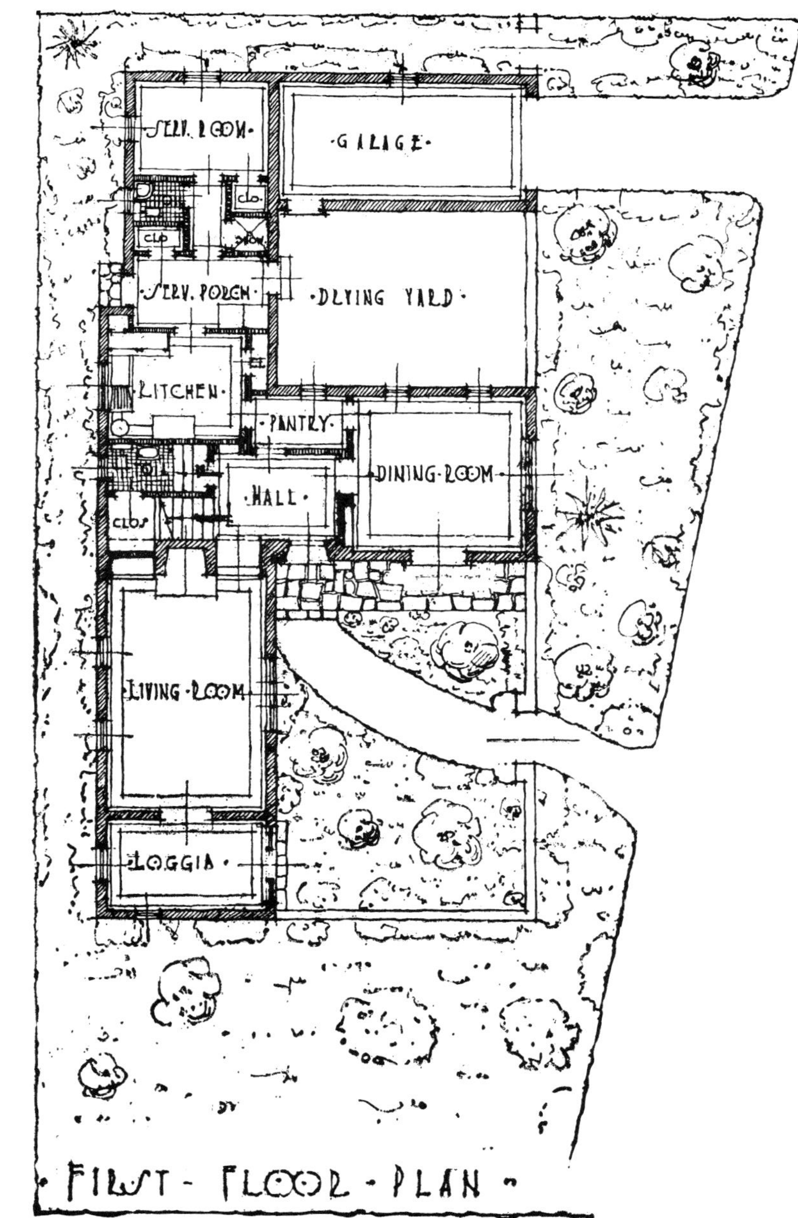

RESIDENCE FOR MR. G. A. MEDCALFE, MIAMI BEACH, FLORIDA

ROBERT L. WEED, ARCHITECT

LIVING ROOM

DINING ROOM

PATIO

RESIDENCE FOR MR. G. A. MEDCALFE, MIAMI BEACH, FLORIDA

ROBERT L. WEED, ARCHITECT

PATIO RESIDENCE FOR MR. ROBERT L. WEED, MIAMI BEACH, FLORIDA
ROBERT L. WEED, ARCHITECT

ENTRANCE DETAIL

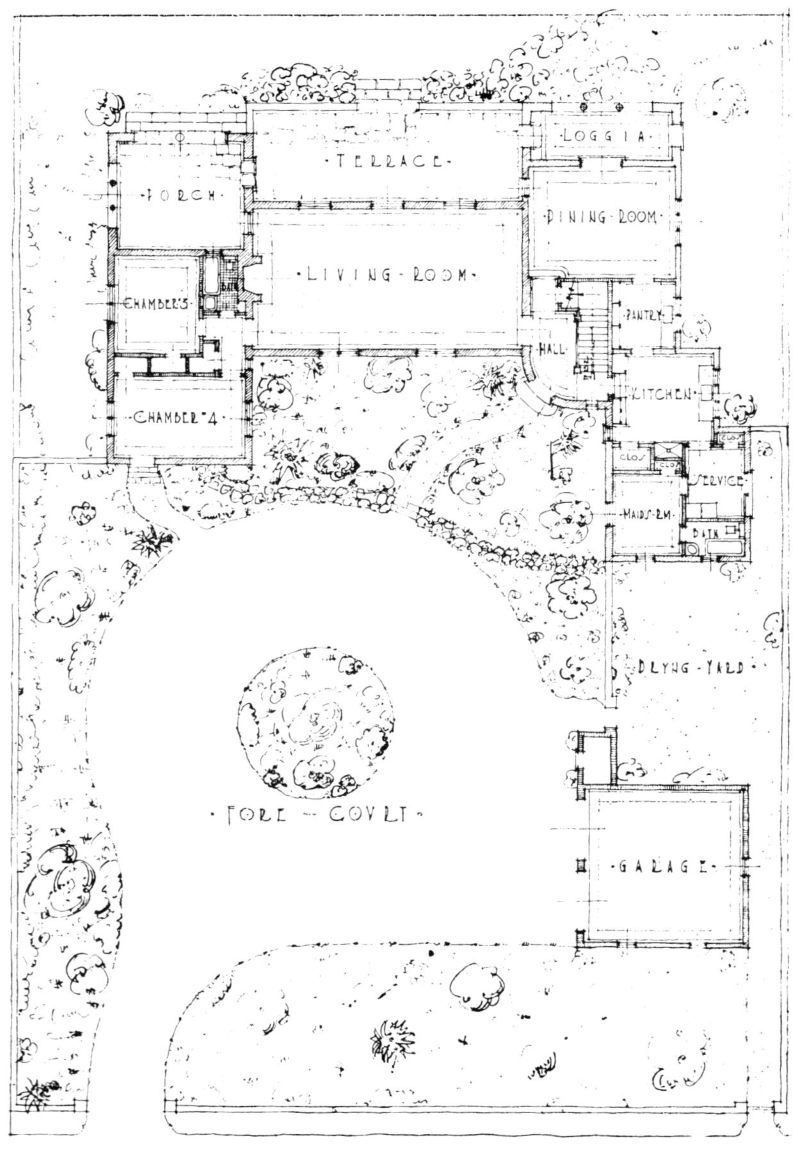

RESIDENCE FOR MR. ROBERT L. WEED, MIAMI BEACH, FLORIDA

ROBERT L. WEED, ARCHITECT

GENERAL VIEW

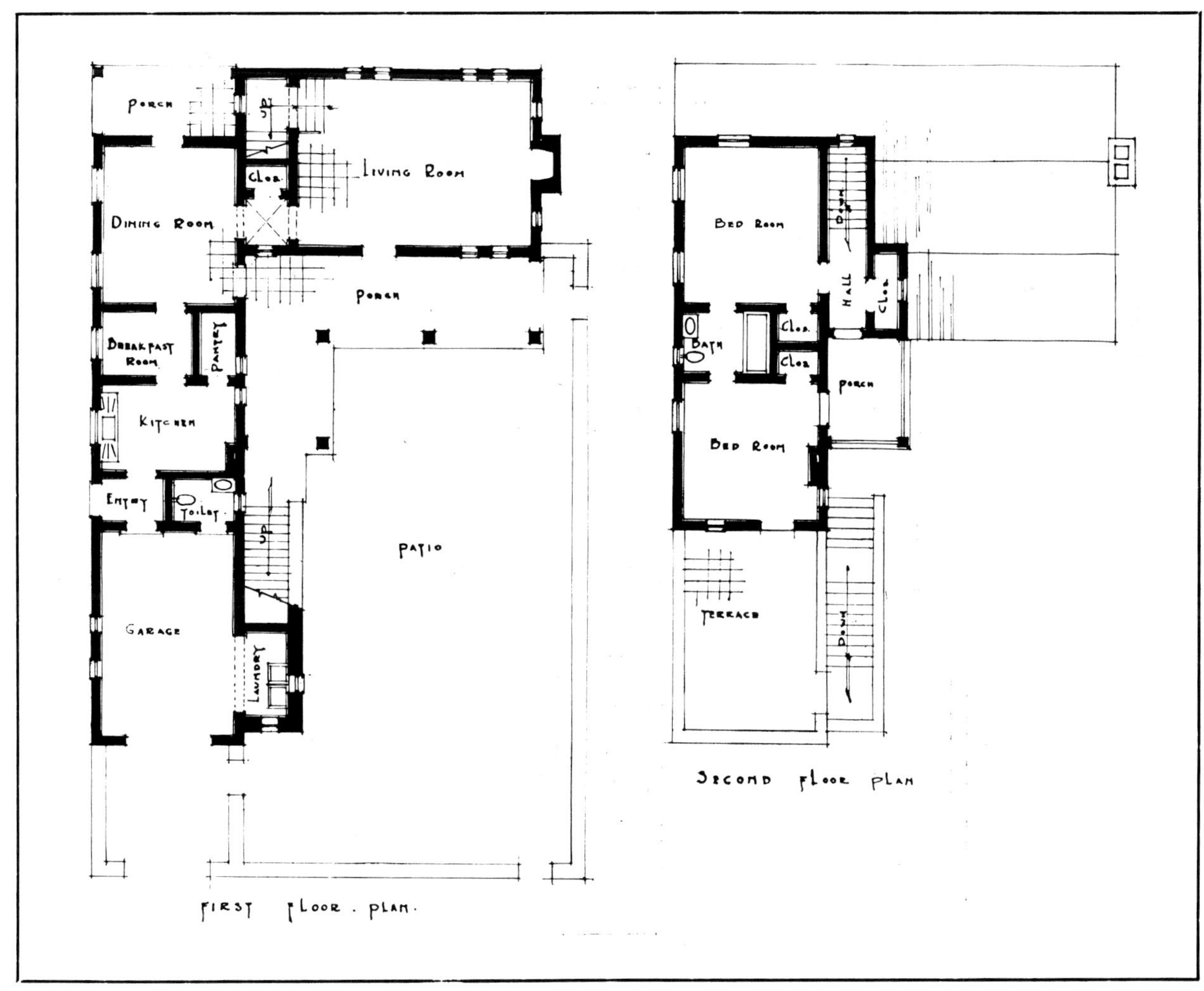

RESIDENCE FOR MR. JOHN L. SKINNER, CORAL GABLES, FLORIDA

JOHN AND COULTON SKINNER, ARCHITECTS

GENERAL VIEW

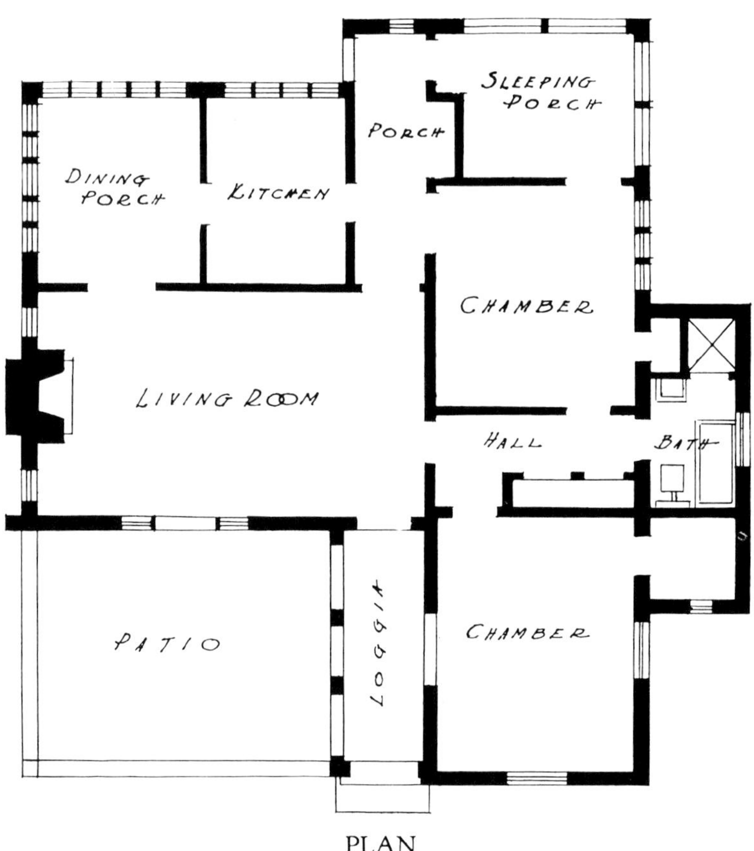

PLAN

RESIDENCE FOR MRS. OTIS SPENCER, CORAL GABLES, FLORIDA

WALTER C. DE GARMO, ARCHITECT

GENERAL VIEW RESIDENCE FOR MRS. CATHERINE ERSWELL, BIRMINGHAM, ALABAMA
WARREN, KNIGHT & DAVIS, ARCHITECTS

REAR VIEW

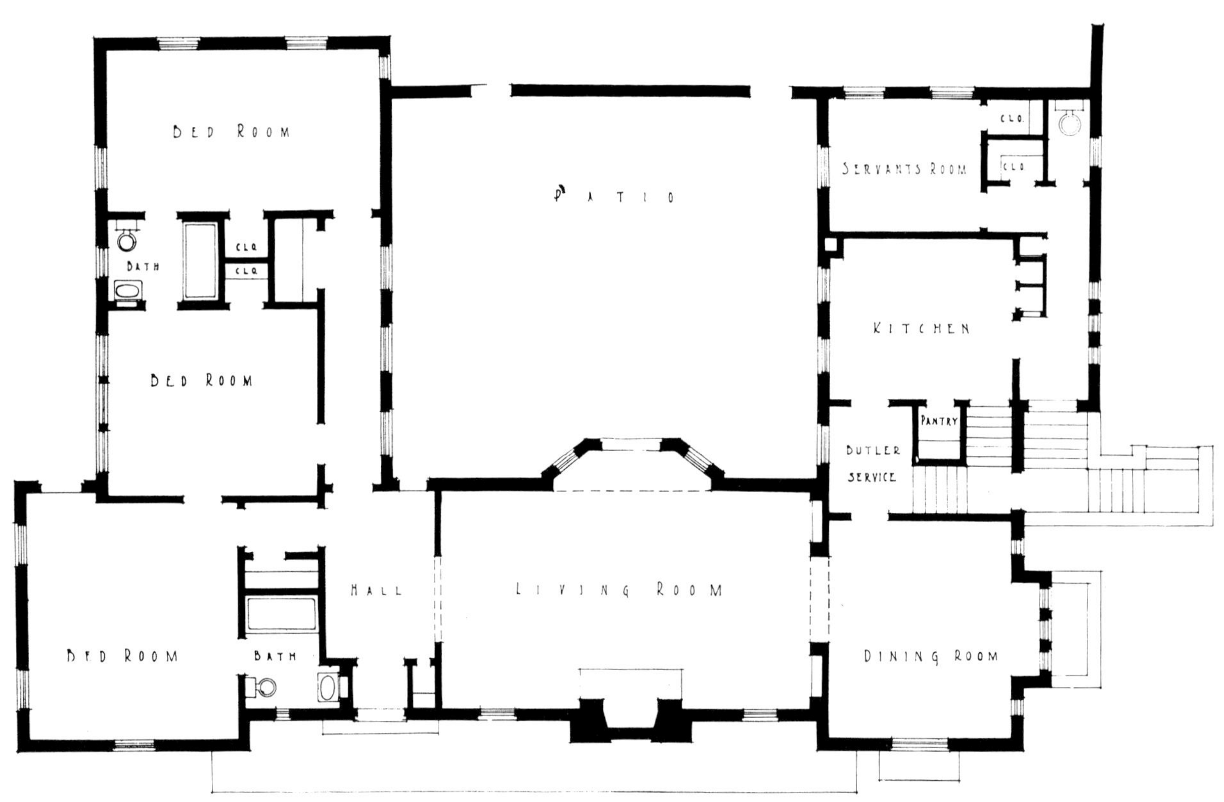

PLAN

RESIDENCE FOR MRS. CATHERINE ERSWELL, BIRMINGHAM, ALABAMA

WARREN, KNIGHT & DAVIS, ARCHITECTS

PATIO

TERRACE

RESIDENCE FOR MRS. CATHERINE ERSWELL, BIRMINGHAM, ALABAMA

WARREN, KNIGHT & DAVIS, ARCHITECTS

DETAIL HOTEL ROLYAT, ST. PETERSBURG, FLORIDA
KIEHNEL & ELLIOTT, ARCHITECTS

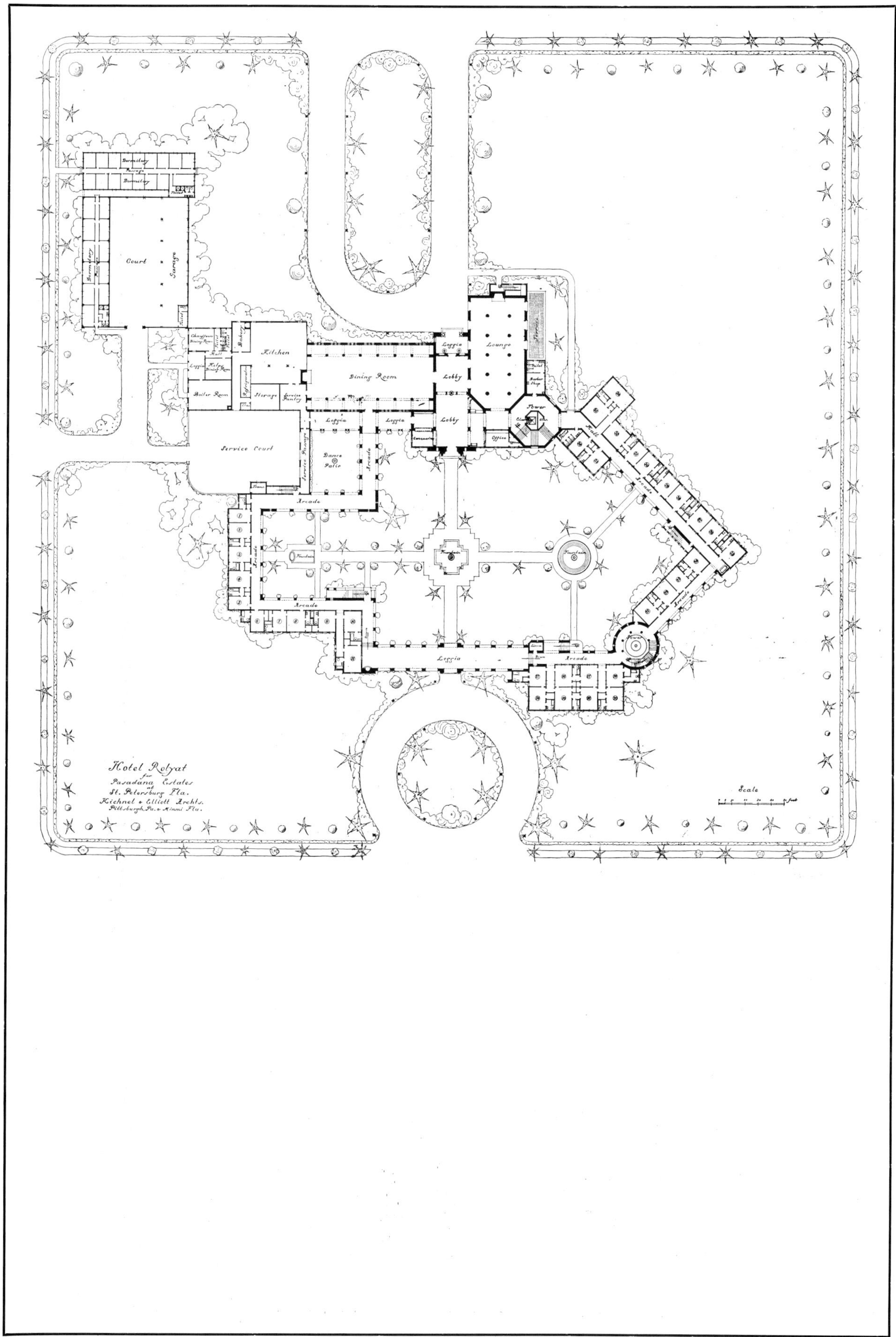

GROUND PLAN HOTEL ROLYAT, ST. PETERSBURG, FLORIDA

KIEHNEL & ELLIOTT, ARCHITECTS

DETAIL HOTEL ROLYAT, ST. PETERSBURG, FLORIDA
KIEHNEL & ELLIOTT, ARCHITECTS

HOTEL ROLYAT, ST. PETERSBURG, FLORIDA
KIEHNEL & ELLIOTT, ARCHITECTS

MAIN ENTRANCE HOTEL ROLYAT, ST. PETERSBURG, FLORIDA
KIEHNEL & ELLIOTT, ARCHITECTS

DETAIL HOTEL ROLYAT, ST. PETERSBURG, FLORIDA
KIEHNEL & ELLIOTT, ARCHITECTS

DINING ROOM HOTEL ROLYAT, ST. PETERSBURG, FLORIDA
KIEHNEL & ELLIOTT, ARCHITECTS

LOBBY HOTEL ROLYAT, ST. PETERSBURG, FLORIDA

KIEHNEL & ELLIOTT, ARCHITECTS

LOUNGE ROOM HOTEL ROLYAT, ST. PETERSBURG, FLORIDA
KIEHNEL & ELLIOTT, ARCHITECTS

DETAIL HOTEL ROLYAT, ST. PETERSBURG, FLORIDA

KIEHNEL & ELLIOTT, ARCHITECTS

PATIO HOTEL ROLYAT, ST. PETERSBURG, FLORIDA

KIEHNEL & ELLIOTT, ARCHITECTS

MAIN ENTRANCE LOBBY HOTEL ROLYAT, ST. PETERSBURG, FLORIDA

KIEHNEL & ELLIOTT, ARCHITECTS